OBERLIN ARCHITECTURE,
COLLEGE AND TOWN
A Guide to Its Social History

OBERLIN ARCHITECTURE, COLLEGE AND TOWN

A Guide to Its Social History

The history of a nation is only the history of its villages written large.

Woodrow Wilson

GEOFFREY BLODGETT

PUBLISHED BY OBERLIN COLLEGE

©1985 by Oberlin College, Oberlin, Ohio 44074
All rights reserved
Library of Congress Catalog Card Number 84-18987
ISBN 0-87338-309-5

Produced and distributed by
The Kent State University Press, Kent, Ohio 44242
First printing designed by Glyphix/KSU

Second printing, 1990

Library of Congress Cataloging in Publication Data

Blodgett, Geoffrey.
Oberlin architecture, college and town.

Includes index.
1. Architecture—Ohio—Oberlin.
2. Oberlin College—Buildings.
3. Oberlin (Ohio)—Buildings.
4. Oberlin (Ohio)—Schools. I. Title.
NA735.03B56 1984 720'.9771'23   84-18987
ISBN 0-87338-309-5 ∞

British Cataloging-in-Publication data are available.

For Dorothy and Harold Blodgett,
my parents, and my sister Mimi

Table of Contents

Introduction

Part One: The College

vii

Part Two: The Town

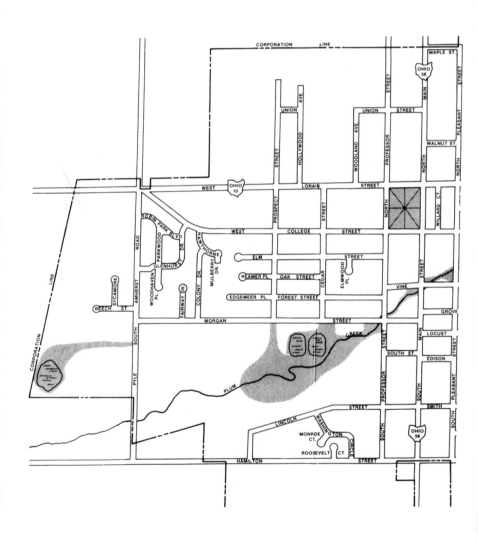

CITY OF OBERLIN

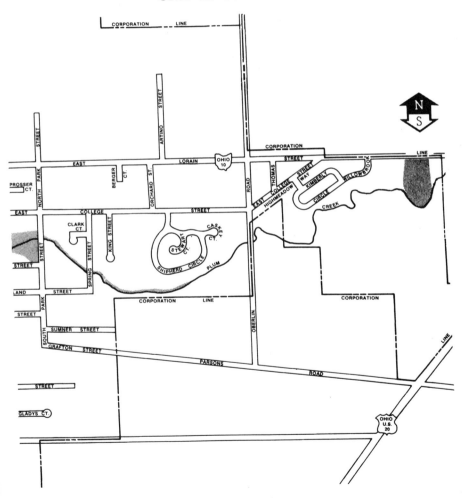

INTRODUCTION
TO 1990 EDITION

Since the completion of this book six years ago, Oberlin architecture ended its long pause and the place has come alive with new construction. True to its past, the college has set the pace. An ornamental bandstand now graces Tappan Square. Its design by Oberlin graduate Julian Smith, a young Canadian architect, won a 1985 international competition initiated by college president S. Frederick Starr. A postmodern addition to North Hall, designed by Peter Saylor of Philadelphia, enhances that once lackluster living space on the college's north campus. Gunnar Birkerts of Birmingham, Michigan, has created a crisply sculptured small, white gem to expand the library space of Yamasaki's Conservatory of Music. New York City architect Charles Gwathmey's elegant new dining facility is in place on North Professor, and a distinctive neuroscience addition, designed by Reed Axelrod of Philadelphia, has risen next to Kettering Hall. Meanwhile, several older college dormitories, as well as many downtown storefronts, have received imaginative renovations faithful to their historic mood. It is satisfying to note these fresh initiatives, while slipping in a few covert corrections to my original text for this reprinting.

June 1990

Oberlinians were different from the outset, self-selected by the special purposes of the place. Those recruited by Oberlin's founder John Jay Shipherd in the early 1830s had to sign his Oberlin Covenant, a stern set of behavioral guidelines for plain living not likely to attract the uncommitted. Thereafter the pivotal role of the college in organizing the community defined the population in other crucial ways. For example, the college decision in 1835 to admit black students, and active local support for the abolitionist movement, made Oberlin a unique haven for fugitive slaves and free persons of color. By 1860 the proportion of blacks among the 2,100 villagers neared 20 percent, and it has grown steadily ever since. These facts fixed Oberlin's regional reputation as surely as its missionary forays farther afield, and helped determine the sorts of people who chose to settle here. Clearly a lot of whites preferred to give the place a wide berth.

Since moral improvement always rivalled intellectual enlightenment in the goals of the college, scrubbing sin from local social arrangements became a major local industry. The dietary reforms of Sylvester Graham's disciples in Oberlin's early years gave way after the Civil War to frequent crusades against billiards, liquor, and tobacco. Each new cause served to tighten the terms of Oberlin's appeal to potential newcomers.

But perhaps as important as any other factor in limiting the pace of village development was the failure to find persuasive reasons for commercial growth. The college cornered the market on industry, and the local population remained relatively small and homogeneous. The community had grown to only 4,300 by 1890. A few prosperous merchants—mostly dealers in groceries, clothing, and drygoods—settled in, and several college faculty members and deacons of First Church enjoyed a reputation for substance as well as status. But nothing answering the description of an "upper class" or a "nouveau riche" mercantile community commanded Oberlin's social structure.

The town therefore lacked what architectural historians regard as a precondition for the showy, imaginative elegance which marked nineteenth-century domestic architecture at its boldest. If the most lavish architectural displays of that age were the advertisements of the rich about their own arrival, Oberlin's chances for sharing in their pride were pretty meager. Nearby examples were not lacking. To the west, the towns of Milan and Norwalk became handsome regional hosts for the Greek Revival on the strength of thriving trade in grain and foodstuffs in the 1840s and 1850s. To the east, Cleveland's opulent Euclid Avenue elite began to cast its shadow in the 1860s, as did Elyria's Washington Avenue residents, more modestly. To the south, a booming cheese industry underwrote the splendid rash of carpenter Gothic, Italianate, and mansard mansions along Wellington's main drives in the 1870s. Through it all Oberlin retained the air of moderate austerity which had marked its building habits since 1833.

Exceptions began to appear in the strident post–Civil War years before and after the depression of the 1870s. Oberlin's famous evangelist, Charles G. Finney, noted these aberrations with grim disapproval. One Sunday morning in July 1870 he lashed out against them in an angry Jeremiad at First Church, condemning his more affluent townsmen for their self-indulgence. "They exult in their good living," his sermon notes record. "Proud of their luxuries. . . . They mind their houses and grounds more than God. . . . As bad as the cities."

What Finney was bewailing was the evidence—houses and grounds—that the simple colony of the 1830s was giving way, however gradually, to some diversity of aims in Oberlin. A high population turnover made up somewhat for slow growth. As the original settlers and their families thinned out, prospering newcomers moved in, and up. Of the 70 richest men in Oberlin in 1865 (according to Civil War income tax returns), barely half were living in town five years before. Though most of them were

xvii

sympathetic with the Oberlin purpose, they felt no great compulsion to self-denial or deference to the local antebellum passions. The changing look of the village reflected the postwar mood. A wave of home improvement swept through. Larger homes, more of them built in brick, with a bit more flourish from the patternbooks, went up along the main new postwar residential streets. Families began to add porches to their homes, and fences and flower plots began to edge their yards. Sandstone sidewalks and carriage blocks went in here and there, quiet assertions of status. White clapboards gave way to a rainbow of new paint tones. "Possibly we are getting a little proud in our old age," the village newspaper editor admitted, "and like to put on a touch of style, now and then—simply to contrast with former poverty, of course."

None of this got out of hand. The great majority of Oberlinians still lived in the angular, gable-roofed, woodframe houses that had set the norms since the 1830s, and most newer homes differed more in size and detail than in kind. Many of them were in fact built big for reasons of economy—to enable owners to round out their income by taking in student roomers from the expanding college.

Oberlin's first substantial architect-designed houses date mainly from the 1890s, before and after the depression of that decade. Thereafter, into the twentieth century to the present, these signature homes served periodically to connect the town to the cosmopolitan world of building fashion, bringing Oberlin abreast of the newness from neo-Tudor to International. But even these stylish arrivals characteristically adapted their flair to the modest expectations of their neighbors. It remained for the campus to register the boldest new departures from its own architectural past. Whatever building adventures awaited the college as it expanded into the new century, it was the destiny of Oberlin itself to remain as it began, a plain and thrifty village, with a population just under 8,500 in 1980.

Of the 40 college buildings on the campus, only three date from the nineteenth century, and none before 1885. If one could punch Fast Forward on a filmtape of Oberlin College's architectural history, the campus might seem like a shooting range of shifting silhouettes, rising up and suddenly collapsing under fire. The college wasted little sentiment on its physical past as distinct from its moral past. The buildings of its first five decades disappeared with hardly any tears, and the relentless process of replacement lasted down through the 1960s. Not until the 1970s did the ethic of preservation and recycling win important converts, and the demolition dust was blown away. Over the long pull, the pace of change on the campus has been much swifter than in the town.

The net deposit is pretty rich, but also variegated and hard to assimilate on a single stroll. The campus is not planless. Rather it is the consequence of successive plans, each launched and partially realized with only limited awareness of those tried out before. They overlapped but didn't quite mesh. The first plan was to build a college on the square, with satellite structures around it, and the faculty lined up on Professor Street. That was the campus of 1885 (though the faculty had scattered early on), cobbled over long years when the college shared the privations of the town.

Then affluence began to hit the college. It came in big gifts from rich men, cultural conservatives who admired Oberlin's moral heritage and, in an income-tax-free age of personal philanthropy, were easily touched to sustain it. Richard Peters, Elbert Baldwin, James Talcott, Lucien Warner, Louis Henry Severance, Andrew Carnegie, and Herbert Wilder were some of their names. The local monument to each stands suitably apart, but together they created the buff gray campus of heavy ashlar sandstone planned for a strong and stately future—the grand march of the stone elephants. That march stopped with World War I.

Meanwhile Cass Gilbert began a long effort, spanning the war by 15 years on either side, to realize his plan for the college, a campus of decorous poise and beauty drawn from inspirations in the European past. The effort ended in the early 1930s in a small storm of rebellion against that past, but Gilbert's grip on the campus remains firmer and more coherent than any other.

Victory in the Second World War ended the long pause dating from the Great Depression and triggered the longest, most frenetic building boom in the history of American higher education. Oberlin College shared fully in this boom, expanding its enrollment from 1,900 in 1940 to 2,500 in 1970. New buildings tumbled off the drawing boards onto their freshly cleared sites, and projects for the next year's campus crowded each other for headlines. Of the college's 40 buildings, 24 went up after 1945. Most of these were dormitories, expedient solutions to meet the postwar student population explosion, and the desire to create a fully residential campus.

This was also the age of Important Architectural Statements, as attention swung from donor, client, and rival plans to the celebrated creative discharge of the architect-as-hero. Most of the Oberlin statements of the age still glow and kindle warm debate. They leave the college community with superb working facilities and a campus appropriate to its end-of-century mood, primed for the heady risks of discontinuity and diversion. Architecturally and otherwise, at Oberlin the status quo remains an irrelevant concept.

A word about the origins of this book may be in order. It began in a search into the local environmental past by a political historian without benefit of training in architectural nuance. Two historians of an older generation, Robert Fletcher of Oberlin and Samuel Eliot Morison of Harvard, informed the search. Morison told us that students of the American past should write not only about stirring events in high places but also about what they can see and touch and hear around them. Fletcher, the preeminent guide to Oberlin's early years, set a standard of academic storytelling for his students and readers that will never be surpassed. He showed us how to do it.

A more immediate inspiration was the drive for historical preservation that swept the country in the late 1960s, more or less simultaneously with the crack-up of this country's political and intellectual arrangements, past and present, which till then had been my main scholarly concern. Assassination, war, and appalling corrosions in our national life tempered my confidence in the sort of history I had learned and practiced, even the history of my ongoing specialty, the political culture of the Gilded Age. As the country's time of troubles wore on, I found the homely stuff of local history and the solid stuff of architectural history more and more alluring as an antidote to great leaders and great thinkers. In retrospect, this seems to have been my private adaption to the new ethic of writing history from the bottom up. The statement quoted at the beginning of this book may no longer have quite the sweep of certitude it had when Woodrow Wilson made it in 1895, but it retains bedrock validity as a place to start in rebuilding one's historical imagination.

Some 130 sketches, arranged in chronological order, make up this survey of college and town. They concentrate on the nineteenth-century village and the twentieth-century campus, though in each case the whole span of Oberlin's history has been considered. Oberlin's small size nourishes the illusion that one might show and tell all there is to know about its architectural past, but the survey does not pretend to be exhaustive. A lot of buildings have been overlooked. Those that are included were chosen for their architectural distinction in some cases, but more often for the vibrant social history they have housed. Some seem very ordinary until this history is known. Out of prudence I have left private homes built since 1950 for later treatment, perhaps by someone else. My sketches are ventures into the social history of architecture at its most eclectic. They are grounded in a belief that buildings help create the environmental fabric in which people make the most important choices of their lives—about shelter, family, politics, money, and self-worth. This book is about those choices. By definition then, I guess, it could go on forever. As a personal project for Oberlin's sesquicentennial year, I decided to end it for the moment now.

Over the past 15 years many Oberlinians have helped me put this book together. Warm thanks go to Dina Schoonmaker, who as a city council member concerned with preservation first suggested back in 1971 that an inventory of important Oberlin buildings be compiled; to Jill Siegel Dodd, a history honors student who spent the summer of 1972 tracing deeds and tax records for me in Elyria and taught me how to do that myself; to Jan Cigliano, an honors student who introduced me to the dense literature on the sociology of space; to dozens of other students in my course in the Social History of American Architecture whose research, enthusiasm, and critical eye have enormously improved my own; to William Bigglestone, a friend with a passion for accuracy and a boundless knowledge of Oberlin history; to his faithful longtime assistant, Gertrude Jacob; to Kenneth Severens, whose expertise in architectural history made him an invaluable guide during his years on the Oberlin faculty; to Robert Longsworth, whose humane wisdom and earthy wit have worked repeated wonders on my morale; to Don Pease, Andy Ruckman, and Dean Howard of the *Oberlin News-Tribune* for their cooperation in this project, which started as a news column; to Barbara Turek and Sandra Chanaca for smooth and patient typing service; to Jeanne West of the Kent State University Press for her meticulous copy editing; and to all the people—homeowners, Oberlin history buffs, and other readers of these sketches—who favored me with help while they were in the making. A special word of gratitude goes to S. Frederick Starr for lavishing his enthusiasm and authority on my efforts to turn the sketches into a book. Last thanks are saved for Jane Blodgett and our children, Lauren, Barbara, and Sally, who put up with this venture on the assurance that it was both important and enjoyable. They sometimes wondered, but never complained.

December 1983

PART ONE:
THE COLLEGE

TAPPAN SQUARE

Known as the College Park or Campus between the Civil War and World War II, Tappan
Square gained its present name through persistent student usage in the 1940s. Although
the name revived early village memories, it
struck some townspeople as "hifalootin, af-
fected and stuffy."

Originally a field of stumps cleared by the first
settlers, the 13-acre square is larger than most
village greens because the founders planned to
build a college on it. Meanwhile, to keep out
vagrant cattle, a worm fence was built to en-
close the space. This gave way to a hedge of
Osage orange which lasted till the early 1880s.

1

Tappan Hall, a combined classroom and dormitory, stood near the square's center from 1835 to 1885, named for Arthur Tappan, a New York City merchant abolitionist who helped Oberlin through many an early financial crisis. The college chapel (1854-1903), Society Hall (1868-1917), French Hall (1868-1927), an octagonal bandstand (1879-1907), and Spear Library (1885-1927) also once graced the square. The last of them were razed according to the will of millionaire alumnus Charles Martin Hall, who admired open park space. This left Memorial Arch, erected in 1903 to honor Oberlin-connected casualties of the Chinese Boxer Rebellion, the only structure on the square, aside from three commemorative boulders which turned into message rocks in the 1960s. While some have felt that its wide expanse, separating college from town where once the two intermingled, compounds local problems of social communication, Tappan Square remains the town's most valuable aesthetic resource. In 1984 Oberlin President S. Frederick Starr laid plans for restoring a festive mood to the square by placing a bandstand on it.

By one count, only two trees stood on the square in 1846. Lavish tree plantings were begun in the 1850s by "students from the East whose life had not been a constant warfare with trees" (in the words of President Fairchild). In 1914 the Olmsted Brothers of Boston introduced a professional landscape program, and the muddy cinder paths and wooden planks of cherished memory gave way to handsome red brick walks. Although the grand arcades of stately elms which once lined these walks disappeared in the 1960s, new plantings have replaced them, and Tappan Square still delights fresh generations of lounging nature lovers with its casual variety.

PETERS HALL
North Professor

A massive stronghold of rough-hewn buff Amherst sandstone, ashlar darkened by age, Peters Hall is the oldest survivor of the spectacular building program which inaugurated the college's stone age in the 1880s. It was the most strident local offering from the Akron architectural shop of Frank Weary and George Kramer, whose stationery called them "specialists in court house, jail and prison architecture." Today the building's appearance is politely labelled Richardsonian Romanesque, and is an acquired taste. Weary and Kramer described it as approximately Gothic, "somewhat domesticated and Americanized," and they were enormously proud of it. "Perfection in this world is acknowledged to be impossible," Weary wrote, "but in the case of your Recitation Hall we feel that we have approached nearer to it than is usual in the history of architectural development." Oberlin shared in the pride. General Jacob D. Cox announced when the cornerstone was laid in July 1885 that Peters marked the end of the era "when beauty in architecture was considered antagonistic to earnest work and good instruction." While some people in later years came to wonder if Peters clinched that precise point, the new hall did assert the post–Civil War architectural virtues of organic stability and bulk.

Money for the building came from Captain Alva Bradley, a Cleveland steamship owner, and a Michigan timber king named Richard Pe-

3

ters, a one-time Oberlin student. It was the first campus building to be equipped with a modern forced-air heating and ventilation system. This made possible its finest interior feature—the big, airy space of the central court. Dressed in red oak oiled woodwork, flooded with afternoon sun, Peters Court became the main campus meeting place for generations of students on their way to class. The place gathered many loyal memories—from those who warmed their hands over the open fireplace through the 1920s, to the bobby-sox dancers of the 1940s, to the antiwar rally organizers of the 1960s. Today the building mainly houses administrative functions spilling over from its neighbor tucked in just to the north.

For over 70 years now, Peters has weathered the desire of influential college planners to tear it down. Gazing at its sturdy dark outline when the moon is up, one suspects it will outlast us all.

TALCOTT HALL
Southwest Corner,
College and
Professor

On this site originally stood the Second Ladies
Hall, a three-story brick dormitory of Italianate
design built during the Civil War. When it
burned in January 1886, the college first
planned to rebuild it using the bricks of the
burnt-out shell. But New York City donor
James Talcott wanted a modern stone building.
Akron architects Weary and Kramer worked
through four sets of plans to get the new hall
just right. The result was impressive—a multigabled ashlar sandstone structure whose proud
porch tower fronting the square is the domi-
nating feature. The round-arched second story
of the porch was originally open to the
weather, a pleasant place for evening sere-
nades. The broad frieze wrapping around the
upper surface of the tower below its conical
roof is repeated across the gabled east and
north walls. Lavish vine and floral carving in
this frieze lends a delicate counterpoint to the
rough texture of Talcott's exterior.

The interior introduced a new grace to Oberlin
dorm life. Rooms were large, well ventilated,
and varied in shape. The woodwork had a
warm and natural finish. In the big first-floor
parlors hardwood floors with figured rugs gave
a fresh look of open dignity. For decades to
come Talcott and her cottage neighbor Baldwin
would underwrite official college efforts to im-
pose refinement on campus social life. In light
of Talcott's long record as a testing ground for
coeducational decorum, its cryptic cornerstone
has inspired many a grin.

5

BALDWIN COTTAGE
South Professor

The construction of Baldwin Cottage, a small-dorm complement to stately Talcott which rose more or less simultaneously next door, began soon after the 1886 fire which destroyed the Second Ladies Hall. It was named for Elbert Baldwin, a Cleveland dry goods merchant from whom Adelia Field Johnston, Oberlin's leading woman administrator, extracted a gift of $20,000.

The village paper announced that Baldwin would be done "in the Queen Anne style, with broken roof lines, with the effect of earlier colonial houses"—language suggesting the wonderfully elastic range of "Queen Anne." Weary and Kramer's design reached for the informal intimacy of a cottage look through variety in massing, texture, and detail. As the walls went up, their odd geometric patterns reminded one observer of an alligator's hide. The studied unexpectedness of Baldwin's shapes—its squat tower, its low double-arched entry porch, the broad and gentle slopes of its roof lines, the episodic placement of its windows and dormers—made it a local triumph in the art of organic irregularity popularized by Henry Hobson Richardson.

The roofing material, a warm red diamond-shaped tile (which has sadly faded over time), introduced a theme that would govern campus building projects for the next 45 years. Here as elsewhere red tile lent a pleasing unity to the completed structure. Dark, rich woodwork

6

helped carry a friendly "nook-and-cranny" mood through the interior, making Baldwin one of the most durably popular living places on the campus.

In 1893 the worst depression of the nineteenth century interrupted the college's intensive building drive. When prosperity returned and the drive resumed at century's end, a subtle shift in architectural taste could be detected in the next wave of construction. Ashlar sandstone remained the characteristic building material, but the new structures moved beyond the bulging complexities of Peters, Baldwin, and Talcott to establish a calmer mood. The restless vertical thrust of the 1880s yielded to more rectilinear and horizontal forms. Warner Gymnasium was the main signal for the shift. Not everyone in Oberlin approved. Chicago architect Normand Patton, Warner's architect and a protagonist of the new aesthetic, had to explain it. "Architectural design in this country has made great strides within the last few years," he wrote, "and in no direction has the improvement been more marked than that of suppressing the height, not for the purpose of making a building look low, but because within the proper limits, a suppression of the height magnifies the breadth, and it is that which gives dignity to a building."

Warner opened in 1901, and the northern section was completed in 1912. The gym was named for its donor, Dr. Lucien Warner, an Oberlin graduate who after practicing medicine in New York City went on to a lucrative career in women's corsetry and spread its dollars on his alma mater. Fred Leonard, the pioneering director of men's physical education, worked

8

closely with Patton to define the facility. The most successful interior components were the big playing spaces on the second floor. Their wood surfaces were hung to give a uniform spring, a trait which 70 years later helped clinch Warner's recycling from gymnastics and basketball to dance.

In 1905, at the outset of his long connection with the college, architect Cass Gilbert decided that Warner was the best of Oberlin's existing buildings and adapted its quiet, round-arched style in his subsequent designs for the campus. The gym itself narrowly survived plans for removal in 1920 and again in 1970. Despite an awkward location, its rugged utility has been hard to deny. In 1983 grounds manager Edward Thompson created a badly needed landscape for the building (renamed Warner Center), punctuated by a concrete dance platform and benches whose octagonal shapes echo the bay in Warner's facade.

9

SEVERANCE LABORATORY
Northwest Corner,
Professor and Lorain

The modernization of scientific training at Oberlin accelerated in 1901. That fall Professor Frank Jewett led his chemistry students, each with an armload of apparatus, in a jubilant march from the cramped rooms of old Cabinet Hall (which stood in decay just south of Peters Hall) to the new Severance Laboratory. Jewett recalled it as a trip from captivity to the promised land. He had spent a sabbatical year examining the latest facilities at universities at home and abroad, and worked closely with young Chicago architect Howard Van Doren Shaw in planning Severance. Money for the new building came from trustee Louis Henry Severance, treasurer of the Standard Oil Company, whose son had studied chemistry under Jewett.

Shaw was just beginning a distinguished career in architecture. He took pride in the exacting craftsmanship and fine detail of his work. His design fitted the tight dimensions of the site and anchored the northwest corner of Tappan Square with a crisp and pleasing sandstone facade. Midway through construction Jewett discovered that some of the interior walls were being lined with overbaked brick. Alarmed, he mailed one of the offending bricks to Shaw, who wired back, "Stop work until I arrive." Shaw came from Chicago by the next train, inspected the scene, and ordered the defective lining rebuilt from scratch. Those were the days.

10

By the late 1950s the attitudes of Oberlin's chemists toward Severance began to echo Jewett's feelings about Cabinet Hall. In 1962 they moved into the new Kettering Hall next door, and Severance was refitted for geology and psychology. The momentum of scientific technology makes it unlikely that the mesh between Severance and its users will ever be as satisfying as it once was for Jewett and his students.

MEMORIAL ARCH
Tappan Square

For many Oberlin graduates Memorial Arch
has symbolized their alma mater's moral
nerve. For others it is a handsome monument
to a lost cause. Dedicated in the spring of 1903,
it commemorates the Oberlin missionaries and
their children who were murdered three years
before in the Chinese Boxer Rebellion, an up-
rising which numbered several hundred west-
erners and many more Chinese Christians
among its victims. Oberlinians had been pursu-
ing the work of Christian education in Shansi
Province since 1882, and were determined that
this bloody setback would not stop their efforts. In 1908 the college formed the Oberlin
Shansi Memorial Association. Its fortunes have
wavered with the surge of revolutionary Chinese nationalism ever since, but it remains
Oberlin's most durable link with the non-

western world. Professor Walter Horton caught what is perhaps the broader affirmation in the arch when he said in 1961 that "if Oberlin should ever cease to produce graduates willing to go out on a limb . . . for new and risky causes on which the state of the world hangs balanced, then it would no longer be Oberlin."

The earliest proposals for the memorial ranged from a simple boulder to a sculpture by Augustus St. Gaudens. Finally the American Board of Foreign Missions, which sponsored the project, decided on a triumphal arch. Built of Indiana limestone embedded with polished red granite panels and discs, it is the only structure on the campus to reflect the formal neoclassicism which swept American public architecture at the turn of the century. The architect was Joseph Lyman Silsbee of Chicago. He is mainly remembered today as the man who in 1887 gave young Frank Lloyd Wright his first year of professional training.

CARNEGIE LIBRARY
Northeast Corner,
Professor and Lorain

Until the 1880s college students rarely used a library for their regular course work. The redefinition of academic scholarship and the advent of electric lighting in the 1890s changed all that. Spear Library (1885) was suddenly obsolete and the college needed a new home for its swelling book collection.

The Cassie Chadwick case, a comic disaster with a happy ending, helped bring Carnegie Library into being. Cassie Chadwick was a clever fraud who conned a local banker out of $350,000 by claiming to be Andrew Carnegie's illegitimate daughter. When her cover was blown, Cassie got ten years, and Carnegie agreed to help out the students who had lost their savings at the bank. Oberlin president Henry Churchill King, who had been negotiating with Carnegie for a new library, spied possibilities in the situation obscure to lesser men. He hurried to New York to convey personal thanks to the millionaire, and came home with the promise of his library.

College librarian Azariah Root shared the planning with Chicago architect Normand Patton, who had done Warner Gymnasium a few years before. Patton's library design, like that of Warner, called for a building of broad, horizontal lines with major facilities located on the second floor. Chief among these was a grand central reading room, for 60 years the main gathering place for college students after dark. The triple gable along the front facade housed

14

windows for top floor seminar rooms. At the
ground level, above a modest entry of vaguely
Egyptian aspect, the pediment is filled with
carved buckeye leaves, echoing one of the trees
that shade it.

Carnegie opened in 1908. Despite a large rear
addition in 1940, it could not keep pace with
implacable space demands and changing assumptions about library design. In 1974 the
huge new Mudd Learning Center superseded
Carnegie. In 1981 the college admissions office
moved in to share the first floor with the town
library. The empty space above, including that
splendid old reading room, entered the 1980s
still waiting for a new career.

15

FINNEY CHAPEL
Southwest Corner,
Professor and Lorain

Finney Chapel was the first of Cass Gilbert's five Oberlin buildings. A correct and gifted architect, Gilbert carved a career of national distinction. His work includes the Minnesota and West Virginia state capitols, the Woolworth skyscraper in New York, and the U.S. Supreme Court building in Washington.

President King chose him to do this memorial to Charles G. Finney, on the site of Finney's Oberlin home, at the suggestion of Finney's son, a western railroader who gave the money for the project. It met the need for a place where the whole college community could come together for academic, religious, and musical occasions. Gilbert struggled for years against interference from the donor and indecision from the college to build it the way he wanted. His plans for the chapel introduced themes he would pursue on the campus over the next quarter-century. Striving for an effect that was "quiet, serious, and strong," he designed it in the round-arched Romanesque church style of twelfth-century southern France. For the exterior walls he chose smooth-cut tan Amherst sandstone, relieved by the red sandstone bands and columns of the great gabled eastern facade, where he concentrated his ornamentation. The interior was simple, even severe. Pews and ceiling were finished in dark stained oak, with piers and trusswork left purposely unadorned to enforce a blunt solemnity.

Gilbert hoped that over future years stained glass, sensitive mural treatment and commem-

16

orative plaques along the inner walls, and a glowing rose window would soften and warm the chapel's atmosphere. Here he misjudged the Oberlin temper, which rarely lingered over the aesthetics of tradition. The building was barely finished in time for commencement in 1908, the seventy-fifth anniversary of the college's founding. Two thousand people gathered in their Sunday best to hear the Musical Union sing the "Hallelujah Chorus" from Handel's *Messiah*. It was a grand moment. Conservatory director Charles Morrison may have chosen this occasion to remark, gazing out over the audience, "Think of it, all this just five miles from Kipton."

In 1982 architect William Blunden, working with an ad hoc college committee and guided by an old presentation wash drawing from Gilbert's office, introduced a new color scheme for the interior while renovating the chapel. This left it closer in appearance to Gilbert's original intentions than it had ever been before.

RICE HALL
West College

Named for longtime conservatory director Fenelon B. Rice and his wife Helen, Rice Hall was built in 1909–10 to complete the facilities of the old conservatory of music, a robust Romanesque pile which once dominated the northwest corner of College and Professor Streets. The architect was A. B. Jennings of New York City, who had designed the main conservatory complex 25 years before.

Rice Hall contained 112 practice rooms, 14 classrooms, and a large first-floor ensemble practice room. The building served other needs from time to time. The first official coeducational social dance in Oberlin College history took place in the Rice basement on Saturday night, 10 January 1920, under the watchful gaze of Mrs. Ellen Birdseye Hatch, director of recreation, the faculty having sanctioned the experiment a month earlier.

Forty years later, when the old conservatory came down to make way for Minoru Yamasaki's new King Building, the decision was made to recycle Rice as a faculty office annex to King. The elaborate fourth-story roof was lopped off to give Rice a proper modern shape, but its dark stone walls remained an uneasy neighbor to Yamasaki's pretty white wedding cake. Folklore has it that when Yamasaki was asked how to soften the incongruity, he replied, "Plant ivy and wait."

Some 75 professors began moving from scattered campus locations into the converted Rice

18

practice rooms in 1963. This centralization of faculty offices in departmental clusters turned Rice into a kind of academic department store. Office doors acquired personalized advertisements and students began to roam the halls, window-shopping for advice and interaction. "Accessibility" became a professorial virtue, although faculty members varied in their terms of accessibility. These ranged from untenured humanistic appeals to drop in anytime to the case-hardened message on the door of one graying social scientist: "Doctors have appointments. Lawyers have appointments. Mechanics have appointments. Administrators have appointments. Businessmen have appointments. And so do Professors! I am available. I am not available on a drop-in basis. See below easy instructions, similar to instructions in the Real World. Prepare yourself for a civilized Afterlife."

**MEN'S BUILDING
(Wilder Hall)
West Lorain**

Throughout Oberlin's history the place of men in the social arrangements of the country's first coeducational college has been a nagging and recurring low-level issue. By the early twentieth century, the formal social life of the campus revolved decisively around women's dormitories, while male students lived in scattered rooming houses all over town. Men's Building, completed in 1911, was supposed to correct this imbalance and create a focus for brotherhood and institutional loyalty among males. "In this stately building," President King hoped, "the college life of the men of Oberlin should take on a dignity and a breadth and a glow of fellowship that it were otherwise difficult to attain." His ideal was a gathering place to help nourish the virtues of "the whole man."

The architect was Joseph Lyman Silsbee, who had earlier designed the Memorial Arch. He planned Men's Building to match the rough-textured look of nearby Warner Gymnasium, Severance Laboratory, and Carnegie Library. The generous proportions of the interior housed dining room, barber shop, billiard room, and bowling alley in the basement; lobby, assembly hall, library, and a "ladies' reception parlor" on the main floor; club rooms on the second floor; and dormitory space for some 65 undergraduate leaders—class officers, athletic captains, editors, literary society officials, and the like—on the top floor. The broad terrace flanking the main entry was designed for rallies and songfests. Few campus buildings reflect so candidly the notion that architecture could shape social behavior—in this case, the collegiate hierarchies, enthusiasms, and amenities of the pre-World War I era.

The anonymous donor who made it all possible was Herbert Wilder, a Boston paper manufacturer who admired the blend of religious concern and academic quality that President King promoted for Oberlin. The building was renamed for Wilder in 1956, long after its function as a male sanctuary was discarded.

Father John Keep ranked among the most re-vered of Oberlin's early patriarchs. He was strong for all the causes that put Oberlin on the map—coeducation, abolition, missionary education. Back in 1835 he cast the tie-breaking vote in the tense trustee decision to admit black students to the college. After that he travelled far and wide to raise money for the place. Then he came home to be father to the college girls who lived and boarded at his home, a wood frame house that stood on this site. He died in 1870. The college bought his house in 1889 and used it as a dormitory for "indigent women students" until 1912. That year the present Keep Cottage went up in its place. Keep's granddaughter, Elizabeth Keep Clark, gave much of the money for the new dorm.

Keep was the last Oberlin commission for Normand Patton, architect of Warner Gymna-sium and Carnegie Library. His charge was to make it a fireproof, homelike residence for 50 women, with pleasant social space on the first floor for mixing with the 30 men who came for meals. Patton first sketched out a Pennsylva-nia Dutch colonial building with stone walls and gambrel roof, but later turned to dark brick and half-timbered stucco which he decided went better with the new Romanesque mood of the campus. He gave the dormitory wide eaves, a broad porch, and big bay windows to create al-coves both indoors and on the porch.

22

Keep remained a women's dorm for the next 55 years. In 1966 it joined the college's flourishing co-op living system.

**COX
ADMINISTRATION
BUILDING
North Professor**

This is the second of Cass Gilbert's contributions to the Oberlin scene. Its construction ended a long intramural struggle over rival visions of future campus development. One faction led by college treasurer James Severance favored the plans of Chicago architect Joseph Lyman Silsbee. These called for a long row of buildings along a north-south axis through the middle of Tappan Square, to screen the college from the town. A large administration building with a walkway passing through it would have centered this design. Blueprints for Silsbee's majestic scheme survive in the college archives.

Influential trustees, including Dudley Allen and Charles Martin Hall and backed by President King, wanted Tappan Square cleared of buildings to create an open park, as recommended by the Olmsted Brothers of Boston, sons of the great nineteenth-century landscape architect, Frederick Law Olmsted. After a decade of quarrelling this view prevailed, but it left the siting of the new administration building unresolved. Gilbert agreed to the ultimate location only in the hope that the incongruous bulk of nearby Peters Hall would soon be removed. His design for Cox advanced his dream for a harmonious campus of mellow, tile-roofed buildings in the style of Mediterranean Romanesque.

The Administration Building was completed in 1915, an inviting sandstone box with elaborate

24

round-arched fenestration and an east entry of uncommon beauty. The building was named for Jacob Dolson Cox, one of Oberlin's most famous graduates, a soldier, politician, and scholar whose traits were symbolized in one of the classical lunettes painted by his son, Kenyon Cox, just inside the entry. The other lunette alludes to Cox's wife, Helen, a daughter of Charles Finney.

Over the years the building's users have had mixed feelings about its somewhat formal and inelastic office space, which has been endlessly remodelled and rearranged. In 1971 President Robert Fuller remarked in an orientation talk to campus newcomers that "the small amount of power in the administration is symbolized well by the size of the Administration Building. It is the smallest building on campus." Fuller's lease on Cox turned out to be very brief. His successors in the building have been making do. The latest of them, S. Frederick Starr, whose fine-tuned enthusiasms include an architectural revival of the campus's older buildings, launched plans for a renovation of Cox which call for restoring the second-floor conference room to its original purpose and installing an exhibit to celebrate Oberlin's Cass Gilbert ensemble.

ALLEN ART BUILDING
Southeast Corner, North Main and Lorain

At the turn of the century the college began to acquire a substantial body of art objects, including the Olney Collection of oils, ivories, and bronzes received in 1904. Meanwhile the art history courses taught by Adelia Field Johnston attracted growing enrollments. The need for an art museum now became apparent. Carnegie Library, Warner Gymnasium and Rice Hall provided space for storage and temporary exhibits until a gift from the estate of Dudley Peter Allen in 1915 promised a finer solution.

Dr. Allen, son of an early Oberlin physician, absorbed a love of art while growing up in the family home (now called Allencroft) on South Professor Street. He graduated from the college in 1875, trained in medicine at Harvard, practiced surgery in Cleveland, and lived in one of Euclid Avenue's fancier mansions. His wife, Elizabeth, was the daughter of oil millionaire Louis Henry Severance, donor of Severance Laboratory. Allen greatly admired Cass Gilbert's Finney Chapel, and consulted steadily with the architect about the museum project through his last years. His widow saw the project through.

Gilbert wanted a building rich in Renaissance associations, yet compatible with the Romanesque mood of his earlier campus compositions. The museum was one of three large structures which he and President King projected for the east side of Tappan Square, the

26

others being Hall Auditorium and a civic center for the town. All three were to be accessible to the public, knitting the college to the surrounding population.

With his customary academic care, Gilbert worked to achieve a warm, alluring building—beauty without monumentality. The low horizontal scale, the deep rhythmic shadows of the arcaded loggia, and the broad overhang of the roof all aimed for this goal. Touches of blue in the rafter extensions of the roof, in the rich frieze, and in the vaulting of the loggia complemented the warm buff and red sandstone patterns of the exterior walls, the red tile roof, and red-brown brickwork of the approach walks. Gilbert worried a bit about the bold color contrasts in this scheme, but assured himself that time and weather would mute its look.

Arrangements inside, with a central sculpture court flanked by galleries and academic work rooms, made for Oberlin's most sumptuous indoor space. And the fountain court to the east of the main block remains a special warm weather delight. Gilbert exercised closer personal control over the museum's construction than in any of his other local commissions, guarding quality in every detail, from the iron grillwork (by Samuel Yellin, at the architect's insistence) to the texture of mortar sand. The building opened in June 1917. Gilbert's Oberlin career here reached its peak.

THE QUADRANGLE
West Lorain

Cass Gilbert's quadrangle for the graduate school of theology was his last effort to give the campus a semblance of visual harmony. For over 20 years he had worked to rescue the college from what a contemporary critic called a "chaos of architectural aberrations," by edging Tappan Square with buildings of settled continuity and appeal. Most of his grand design for Oberlin was never realized. Even his final installment came slowly.

Gilbert's preliminary drawings for the quadrangle date from 1919. They gathered dust for a decade while the college looked for the money to act on them. Finally a $400,000 gift from the Rockefellers, supplementing an earlier bequest by D. Willis James, launched construction in 1930. The quadrangle replaced old Council Hall, an angular neo-Gothic structure condemned by both the state of Ohio and Gilbert's taste. (Council Hall had been built in 1874 next to the former home of Oberlin's founder, John Jay Shipherd.)

The details in the new theological complex were mostly the work of Eugene Ward, a young architect in Gilbert's office who relied on sketches from the aging master. The quadrangle was designed to provide divinity students with a small campus of their own, complete with chapel and library, classrooms, faculty offices, dining hall, gymnasium, and living space, all surrounding a quiet green interior yard.

28

Bosworth Hall, built of Indiana limestone, fronts the Square with a central Romanesque tower and hand-carved medieval doorways. Fairchild Chapel, also of limestone, projects northward from the tower's base into the yard. Shipherd Hall, finished in dark red brick, encloses the complex on the north. Brick dormitory wings flank the yard on either side, connected to Bosworth by arcaded limestone colonnades. The capitals of the west colonnade are decorated with the carved faces of notable men in Oberlin's history—a rare effort to relate architectural ornament to the local past. When someone asked the architect's son what the quadrangle's style was, he tartly replied that "the stonework was American, the character was based on Northern Italy, and the style was 1930 Cass Gilbert."

In 1965, with an eye to hard secular realities, college trustees voted to close the graduate school of theology, and the quadrangle was recycled to meet new needs. Bosworth became an administrative annex and Shipherd was converted into Asia House. The cool recesses of Fairchild Chapel (whose stained glass windows, by Henry Lee Willet, were not installed till 1959) survive as the main reminder of the quadrangle's original purpose.

NOAH HALL
Woodland

On campuses all over the country in the 1920s,
attention turned to providing more adequate
living arrangements for men. Harvard's house
system and Yale's college plan were the most
ambitious projects along this line. At Oberlin,
despite the opening of Men's Building in 1911,
the problem seemed especially urgent. By the
mid-twenties, the overwhelming majority of
male students lived in some 200 private rooming houses off campus. Most of these places
housed groups of four or five. Many more had
solitary roomers.

In 1928 the trustees decided this was unaccept-
able. They resolved that "Oberlin shall have a
Men's Campus on which the men shall live together in buildings owned and operated by the
College, a campus on which the life of men can
be organized and developed in such a way as to
stimulate scholarly ambition and create an active masculine social atmosphere." Quaint
words.

Trustee Andrew Noah, an Akron rubber manufacturer, promised $100,000 to help realize the
dream, and a student-faculty committee
chaired by Dean Edward Bosworth launched a
thorough study of needs and possibilities. The
upshot was a plan for a quadrangle of 13 new
dorms, all in the red-brick neo-Georgian
manner popularized by Colonial Williamsburg.
Bounded by North Professor and Woodland
streets, the new men's campus would lie between a prospective science complex to the

south and athletic fields to the north. These linkages were supposed to enforce the male priorities of the new environment.

The Great Depression then intervened. Noah Hall was the only unit of the plan to go up before the Second World War. Designed by Akron architect C. W. Frank and completed in 1932 under great financial duress, Noah remains architecturally the most carefully finished of Oberlin's dormitories. Art professor Clarence Ward had charge of the interior decor and furnishings for rooms and lounges. Together with its neighbor Burton Hall, completed in 1947, Noah stands as a reminder of a lost moment in campus planning when Georgian dignity seemed to control an important future. The concept of a men's campus disappeared in the 1960s.

HALES GYMNASIUM
West Lorain

Women's athletics at the college have come a long way from prim and primitive beginnings. The first women's gym was a tiny frame building, originally called Music Hall, which was converted into a place for female exercise in 1874. It stood on the present site of Baldwin Cottage until it burned in 1880. Its successor was built a year later on land just west of Talcott Hall. A skating rink donated by John D. Rockefeller was added to this in 1895.

Meanwhile Delphine Hanna, who came to Oberlin to direct the gym in 1885, was transforming conventional attitudes about women's athletic capabilities. Dr. Hanna acquired an M.D. from the University of Michigan in 1890 and became professor of physical training in 1903. While helping to promote the idea that physical education was an academic discipline, she also worked to expand female physical activity beyond dance and gymnastics to include such competitive team sports as tennis and basketball.

By the 1930s the old women's gym looked and smelled medieval. Remedies began with the building of Crane Pool in 1931, largely financed by a gift from Mr. and Mrs. Winthrop Crane, whose daughter Barbara graduated from the college in 1930. The architect was another Oberlin graduate, Claude Stedman in the Cleveland firm of Walker & Weeks.

Hales Memorial Gymnasium, named for donor George W. Hales and designed by New York architect Richard Kimball, opened in 1939. It brought the first tentative expression of "modern" to the campus, reflecting as it did the influence of the airplane hangar on gymnasium design. Its smooth facade of Indiana limestone is an uneasy marriage of classical symmetry and functional simplicity. The low, flat lines of the 1958 bowling alley addition to the east, designed by Oberlin graduate Herk Visnapu, completed the eclectic three-part complex.

When Philips gymnasium opened in 1971 and coeducation arrived in physical education, the bulk of the women's program migrated to the new facility, leaving Hales in a state of underemployment. As elsewhere, architecture continues its struggle to stay abreast of fast-changing educational assumptions.

**WRIGHT PHYSICS
LABORATORY
North Professor**

In architectural history the gap between visions projected and reality achieved is often big. So it was with the college's science quadrangle, an ambitious plan of the late 1930s. Almost four decades had passed since chemistry had moved into Severance Laboratory. Zoology occupied an abandoned church, physics was trapped in Peters basement, and geology and botany struggled along in converted woodframe houses. Oberlin's scientists were restless.

Guided by architect William Hoskins Brown of the art department, who admired the interlocked building arrangements for the sciences at his alma mater, M.I.T., they came up with a scheme for a vast U-shaped complex on the north campus facing West Lorain Street. They hoped their plans would adapt to changing growth rates among the sciences (including math and psychology), while exploiting interdisciplinary overlap and needs for shared equipment. Brown later recalled that the science faculty's support for his ideas was virtually unanimous.

In 1940, Brown having left Oberlin, Cincinnati architect E. J. Schulte was asked to prepare plans for the quadrangle. His "modified Romanesque" designs for two of its components, physics and biology, were approved in 1941, though Brown's colleague in the art department, Clarence Ward, questioned Schulte's command of the Romanesque and favored a Georgian style more compatible with the projected men's campus to the north (another failed dream).

America's entry into World War II restricted construction to the physics unit. It opened in February 1943, just in time to accommodate the wartime V-12 navy students who arrived the next summer. The building—the last in Oberlin's round-arch, red-tile roof tradition launched with Baldwin Cottage 55 years before—was named in honor of the Wright brothers, Wilbur and Orville, in 1948.

The war, faculty turnover, a change in presidents, and emergency postwar dormitory needs combined to send the integrated science complex into limbo. The anomalous red brick wall patches on Wright Laboratory, anticipating future points of connection with other units, survive as testimony to the hope.

JONES FIELD HOUSE
North End of
Woodland

Jones Field House, erected in 1948, is the last relic of several war surplus buildings that dotted the campus after World War II. Most of them arrived through the work of the Federal Public Housing Authority to help the college cope with the flood of veterans returning under the G.I. Bill.

Enrollment rose to a new high at war's end—over 2,000 in the fall of 1946, 800 of them veterans. Makeshift rooming space was set up for the overflow in Warner Gymnasium and in attics all over town. Thirty men slept temporarily in the auditorium of Men's Building (now called Wilder Main Lounge). Fifty trailers for married veterans and their wives stood for several years on the campus just north of West Lorain Street in a muddy, cheerful eyesore called Botany Lane. North of that next to Noah Hall, a prefabricated war workers dormitory from Willow Run, Michigan was installed in 1947, sprawling out in several odd directions from its core. Named Federal Hall, it acquired the nickname "Spider." Meanwhile a large men's cafeteria, imported from an army ordnance depot in Sandusky, went up just south of the present site of Mudd Learning Center. By 1956 all of these had disappeared.

The Field House, named for former college secretary George M. Jones, was a wartime navy drill hall from Camp Perry, Virginia. Architect Eldredge Snyder supervised its adaption as an athletic space and designed the lobby and team rooms connecting the Field House to the stadium. A moveable wooden floor over the dirt surface, closely surrounded by stands seating 1,800, made the Field House a snug home for college basketball games from 1948 to 1971. It was the scene of many memorable events, including the winter night in 1970 when coach Julian Smith made the substitution that put five black players on the floor for Oberlin. Old-timers among the fans sensed the meaning of the moment but wondered how to respond. Black students in the crowd had no trouble. They broke into a rousing chant: "All Black Team! All Black Team! All Black Team!" Oberlin won. Two years later, the team had moved into Philips gym, the Jack Scott "athletic revolution" got under way, and Smith was replaced as basketball coach by Olympic sprinter Tommie Smith.

The Field House today is less familiar to most people than its neighbors. The stadium to the east was constructed in 1925. To the west is the Williams Rink for ice skating and hockey, installed in 1963.

When Hall Auditorium opened in 1953, the *Cleveland Plain Dealer* called it "the most controversial building in Ohio." Later entries on the campus scene have muted that controversy, but opinions still clash over Hall—its size, appearance, and utility. Since these issues swirled around the building for 40 years before its actual construction, the auditorium merits the *Plain Dealer*'s judgment if only for the sheer longevity of the quarrel. No building project anywhere better reflects the turmoil in the world of architectural politics since World War I.

That war had just broken out when Charles Martin Hall willed $600,000 for "a large auditorium" in memory of his mother, to be used by both college and town to encourage "all forms of education." Hall named Cass Gilbert as the desired architect and Cleveland lawyer Homer Johnson as the trustee of his will. President King promptly clamped a religious definition on the building, hoping it would become a common place of worship for all the Protestant churches in town, while also serving as a concert hall. He imagined an auditorium seating 4,000, with a basement theater accommodating 800 more.

Gilbert's first sketch for the project dates from 1915. His proposed facade was a more elaborate version of his Finney Chapel across the square. The war and then postwar inflation delayed its construction, but in 1928 college trustees decided to build. Then came the Great Crash.

38

Hall's gift (invested in slumping Alcoa stock) no longer supported King's vision or Gilbert's design. Homer Johnson, whose son Philip was just emerging as a proponent of the modern International Style, balked not only at Gilbert's plans, but at those of four succeeding architects, including the distinguished Eliel Saarinen. In later years Johnson cheerfully confessed the hope that his son would be the ultimate designer.

In 1946, incoming president William Stevenson, a lawyer by profession, moved to resolve the impasse. In collaboration with architect Eldredge Snyder, his Princeton classmate and friend, he settled with Homer Johnson on Philip Johnson's friend Wallace Harrison, chief designer of the United Nations complex in New York City. When Harrison's plans came in well over cost, the college filed a successful suit in 1951 to reinterpret Hall's will and make possible what Stevenson called "the best little jewel of an auditorium with the money available." In process, the original projected 4,000-seat capacity shrank to just over 500.

Harrison's final design was stunning. The curving flow of its limestone walls and the tall, undulating white marble curtain facing the street offset the cubist massing of the stagehouse and give the building a more monumental look than its size sustains. Some thought it matched the campus ambiance with all the grace of a beached whale, and dubbed it Moby Dick. But its expressive theatrical beauty, enhanced by fine landscaping, has won many converts, who only wish it had more seats.

THE OBERLIN INN
Northeast Corner,
College and Main

When the present Oberlin Inn replaced its 87-year-old predecessor in 1955, the town's main intersection was radically transformed and "motel moderne"—a low budget adaption of the flat-roofed International Style—arrived in Oberlin.

The inn is the fourth hotel to occupy the site and lends continuity to the town's long tradition of plain living for its guests. Brewster Pelton launched the tradition in 1833 with a small log cabin that included space for "strangers." Two years later he built a larger frame hotel. When this burned in 1866 it was replaced in 1868 by the three-story brick hotel that lasted till 1954, providing visitors in college secretary Donald Love's words with "mid-Victorian charm and a certain frontier indifference to baths." Marx Straus, Oberlin's rich immigrant clothing merchant, deeded this building to the college in 1895.

Around the turn of the century, the hotel combined with its neighbors to provide the village with a main crossroads of authentic urban vitality. Brick business blocks walled the sidewalks on three corners; a village bandstand near the Historic Elm enlivened summer shopping crowds with music and pranks; popcorn and candy stands did a thriving corner business; and electric interurban trolleys pumped people in and out of town in large numbers. Psychologically, Oberlin was closer to big-city America than it ever has been since.

But as early as 1914 plans were underway for major change. Charles Martin Hall, Henry Churchill King, and architect Cass Gilbert laid plans for a new complex on the hotel site—a multipurpose community civic center surrounding a modern inn and restaurant. Two world wars and the Great Depression killed that project.

The inn, completed in 1955, designed by Eldredge Snyder under tight cost constraints imposed by college trustees, substituted brick, glass, and cinderblock austerity for the sagging charm of its predecessor. A warmer, more handsome, and nicely appointed east addition, designed by Joseph Ceruti and completed in 1970, vastly enhanced the inn's appeal.

The years following World War II coincided with the decisive onset of architectural modernism and marked a major turn in campus architecture. President William Stevenson, startled on his arrival in 1946 by the college's haphazard student housing, launched a dormitory building program which outlasted his tenure and continued down through the term of his unlucky successor, Robert Carr. These were years of fast growth in academic America. Here as elsewhere the dorms that went up were often expedient, undistinguished structures— quick solutions to urgent needs. When one recalls the dozens of aging wooden houses torn down to make room for them, they can be called Oberlin's campus version of urban renewal.

Dascomb, a long, flat slab of sleeping space with a big lobby and dining hall attached, serves to illustrate the problem and the response. Together with its fraternal twin, Barrows, on the north campus, it signalled an abandonment of the Georgian amenities hoped for by prewar dormitory planners. Inflated building costs, together with the stringent loan requirements of the U.S. Housing and Home Finance Agency, enforced the shift toward a horizontal, collectivized version of the spartan "plain-style" that had governed so much private nineteenth-century housing in the town.

Dascomb and Barrows, which were filled with students in 1956, came from the drawing

42

boards of a Cincinnati firm, Potter, Tyler, Martin & Roth. Seven years later this firm returned to bestow South Hall and East Hall on the campus. By then a concerted student protest had blown up against big-dorm anonymity. This protest was the main medium by which the anger of the 1960s arrived in Oberlin. "Dascomb" had become a "dirty word," one junior Phi Bete solemnly announced, "a symbol for triviality and intellectual sterility." Demands intensified for smaller, more decentralized and intimate living arrangements. The last phase of dorm construction, 1966–68, tried to meet these desires. Some half dozen buildings of modest scale, called "interest dorms," were the result.

Now that the campus building boom is past history, the college is working to make all its modern dormitories more livable and interesting, inside and out.

**KETTERING HALL
OF SCIENCE
West Lorain**

Oberlin's most modern science building, named for the inventor Charles F. Kettering, houses biology and chemistry. It originated as a quick, functional resolution to a small 1950s cold war between the college and the country's most prestigious architectural corporation. The college got what it finally wanted from this contest, except the glamor of a Skidmore, Owings & Merrill label for the campus.

In 1957 Oberlin commissioned S.O.M. to produce a building that would meet long-standing science needs postponed by World War II. The plan developed back in the late 1930s to meet these needs, an integrated quadrangle for all the sciences, had gotten waylaid in the interim. The college now called for a single rectilinear building facing West Lorain Street, and asked for a design highlighting aluminum, to honor Charles Martin Hall and peg fund raising. The response from S.O.M. was a comprehensive disappointment, offering a long, sleek glass box, poorly adapted to local desires and promising high operating costs. One caustic critic said that the presentation drawings made it look like something expensive squeezed from a tube. Though startled by Oberlin objections to the plans and price tag, S.O.M.'s New York office could not make its vaunted design system yield satisfactory modifications. The corporation's star designer, Gordon Bunshaft, fresh from Lever House and other international triumphs, seemed especially aloof to college negotiators. A long standoff ensued.

44

Meanwhile fund raising for the project prospered, as big gifts came in from the Kettering and Rockefeller Foundations. Impatience mounted among administrators and faculty scientists. The deadlock was broken when college trustees turned to the Austin Company, a construction firm headed by trustee George Bryant, for an alternative. This saved over half a million dollars and a lot of time. By July 1961, Kettering Hall of Science was in place—engineered, approved, built and fitted out in less than a year. The Austin Company's headquarters building in Cleveland provided the prototype.

Kettering's workplace efficiency and no-nonsense look, dramatized by its painted steel H-beam columns, steel-blue brick, and hard, flat, white cornice, spoke "science" to the campus. In the end there was little aluminum in the structure, and less poetry. But so far it has succeeded in meeting the stern demands of its users.

CONSERVATORY OF MUSIC
Southeast Corner, College and Professor

In 1956 architect Douglas Orr was asked to produce a long-range program for modernizing the teaching façilities of the college. The Orr Plan proposed to concentrate most college activity in the quadrangle west of Tappan Square and relocate the conservatory of music along the square's southern edge. To make way for change, Orr also called for a startling program of demolition. Severance, Peters, Warner Gymnasium, Rice, Talcott, Baldwin, Allencroft, and Johnson House would all have long since disappeared if the Orr Plan had been fully realized. The plan hit the press in 1957.

As with most master plans in Oberlin's history, backlash followed fanfare, and piecemeal eclecticism triumphed. The main consequence of Orr's suggestions was the arrival of Minoru Yamasaki's additions to the campus scene. The big disappearance was Warner Hall, the old conservatory dating from the 1880s, judged to be an obsolete firetrap.

Old Warner, a vast organic sandstone pile which stood south of Peters, was in fact no longer adequate for a music school rivalling Juilliard and Eastman. In Yamasaki's new conservatory, the various functions crammed in the old complex were sorted out and rearranged in an attractive new ground plan kitty-corner across the street. Those who negotiated with Yamasaki recall that he had studied the spatial problems well and was a superb salesman for his final design. Construction

46

lasted from 1961 to 1964. The first unit to open was the practice building, a nicely organized facility named for David Robertson, the conservatory director who was the moving force behind the drive for the new complex.

Yamasaki's conservatory has inspired praise and headaches ever since. Aesthetically, its chief virtue is its glistening beauty as a thing-in-itself, viewed from a distance on a sunny day. Its repetitive white rhythms, a characteristic Yamasaki blend of modern Gothic and classical allusions, went with nothing else in Oberlin. Delicate and pretty in appearance, the steel-reinforced quartz-aggregate facades have proved to be fragile shells for their inhabitants. Poor communication among architect, contractors, acousticians, and client produced a medley of construction flaws that would seem laughable but for the unending costs involved in fixing them. Bibbins Hall, the main office and teaching unit fronting the square, has required extensive weatherproofing and structural repairs. Meanwhile the acoustical disappointments in Warner Concert Hall provoke constant debate and still await satisfactory remedies.

Twenty years after its completion, the conservatory complex apparently faces a future of steady remedial improvement if it is to last. The lovely oriental garden landscape facing Professor Street has somehow proved more durable than the buildings that frame it.

KING BUILDING
Northwest Corner,
College and
Professor

Henry Churchill King served Oberlin College
as president longer than anyone else, from
1902 to 1927. He is remembered (somewhat
nostalgically) as the last man to lead a harmonious community in Oberlin—town and gown,
faculty and students. The records of his tenure
verify his reputation for remarkable powers of
personal persuasion, which commanded loyalty
if not always consent. The humane, full-
rounded education of the whole person was his
constant academic goal. King Building, which
replaced Peters and Westervelt Hall as the college's main classroom building for humanities
and social science, was intended to honor
King's ideals and achievements 30 turbulent
years after his death.

In the planning, siting, and construction of the
memorial, it yielded priority to the new conservatory of music, a more complex project by
the same architect, Minoru Yamasaki. King
Building went up over a six-year span beginning in 1959 on the site of the old conservatory,
and before that, the site of the home of Asa
Mahan, Oberlin's first president. The two
main stages of the building process are marked
by the subtle difference in the neo-Gothic grillwork applied to its northern and eastern facades. Early on in the building's history, a section of this grillwork fell off. One hopes this
was an aberration. The conversion of sturdy
old Rice Hall just to the west from a music
practice building into a faculty annex was a
prudent cost-saving measure, but it deprived

48

King of the architectural autonomy which Yamasaki's dainty style called for.

Despite its blank main entry, cramped stairwells, and false symmetries, the building works well as a teaching facility. How President King might react to the clatter of rival facts and opinions ricocheting through its classrooms is anybody's guess.

**PHILIPS PHYSICAL
EDUCATION CENTER
Woodland**

Robert Carr presided over two major building projects across the 1960s, in addition to the dormitories large and small that sprouted all over the place in those years—a big new library and a big new gym. Though his presidency stopped before either was completed, he took special satisfaction in the Philips Physical Education Center, whose progress he oversaw more closely than any other. Architectural judgment was not Carr's strong suit, but the Philips gym was a success he worked hard for, along with the donor, trustee Jesse Philips, and the local planning coordinator, longtime physical education chairman Lysle Butler. On balance, no recent campus building has brought more satisfaction to its users. The complaints have mainly come from those left out.

When planning got underway in 1963, no one doubted that a replacement for Warner Gymnasium, a building geared to basketball and Swedish gymnastics, was overdue. The modern stress on honing individual sports skills and personal fitness was built into Philips from the outset. So was an awareness that the college could benefit in its search for male applicants from a more attractive athletic plant. The new gym's squash and swimming facilities promised to make it a regional center for tournaments in these sports, and the big multipurpose playing space for basketball, volleyball, and tennis, equipped with moveable stands, was calculated to encourage broad intramural participation in indoor team sports.

50

Planners made one large mistake. They
missed the coming surge in women's
athletics and the integration of male-female
physical education, which turned out to coin-
cide exactly with the gym's construction in
1969–71. Coeducational gymnasiums were
not a new idea. Clarence Ward had suggested one for Oberlin as early as 1937. Midway through the planning for Philips, Carr
urged more attention to women's locker and
shower space, but the issue did not surface
as a major concern until the building opened.
Hasty patching after that never quite caught
up with demand. Town access to the gym by
teen-agers and adults proved to be another
nagging problem, as the college strove to
dodge the stigma of elitism. The building's
social politics have been much more complex
than its sponsors bargained for.

Architect Hugh Stubbins came into the planning process in 1964. His firm's solution to
the program presented to it was by all
accounts smooth and competent, aside from
the inevitably leaking flat roof. The building,
for all its vast rectangular sprawl, rests
unobtrusively on its site and makes a handsome neighbor for the main campus. The
alternating rhythm of warm brick diamond-
shaped piers and dark glass along the Woodland facade calls to mind the words Cass
Gilbert used to admire old Warner Gymnasium back in 1905: "serious, quiet and not
extravagant."

The college spent 15 years, spanning three presidencies, edging crablike toward the decision to build Mudd Learning Center the way it is and where it is. Most academic people believe that the library is the crucial center of the learning enterprise. By the 1950s many worried that Oberlin's library facilities were decomposing at the core. President Stevenson's hope that Carnegie might be renovated and expanded one more time was scrapped in 1963 when consultant Ralph Ellsworth recommended that a new library be built on the quadrangle west of Tappan Square. This inspired one last hurrah for Cass Gilbert's grand design of 1914, an architectonic campus plan that would connect Hall Auditorium in a long east-west sight line across the square to a climactic monument somewhere beyond the Memorial Arch. By 1967 the New York City firm of Warner, Burns, Toan & Lundy produced an imperial library design appropriate to this scheme. Peters Hall and Warner Gymnasium, obstructions to the plan, entered the endangered list, and trustees approved Warner's demolition while accepting a major grant from the Seeley G. Mudd Foundation for the library. Inclusion of computer and audiovisual facilities qualified the new building for the expansive label, Learning Center.

In 1970, as the Carr presidency gave way to Robert Fuller, the college entered a final spate of reassessment about the cost of a huge new central library and the wisdom of destroying so much to plant it in the space behind Peters. Friends of the older buildings rallied behind the advice of consultant Arthur Drexler, who told Fuller, "There is little to recommend a college concerned with the humanities if it substitutes 'improvement' as a euphemism for the vandalization of its own history." Finally the decision was made to spare Warner and Peters, and move Mudd's site northwest to its present location close to Wilder and the Service Building. This kept "Wilder Bowl" open and made it a primary intersection in the campus traffic flow, which for most of the past century had strung out along Professor between Talcott and Carnegie. Wilder became Mudd's social annex, and the Service Building gave Mudd something architectural to relate to. A landscape plan devised by Dan Kiley to screen Mudd from other campus buildings with dense tree plantings while introducing a big saucer-like depression in front of Mudd was fortunately abandoned in deference to Oberlin's climate and geology.

Not very much was done about the proposed design for Mudd itself except to build it, a task that lasted three years. The spatial interpenetrations of its eastern face, with receding scholars bridges stretched above a long-tongued entry ramp, borrowed some dramatic French ideas from the 1950s, and reminded historian Barry McGill of a stage set for the entombment scene in *Aida*. By the time the building opened in 1974, campus critics were reconciled to its colossal outdoor mass of limestone and glass, and prepared to exploit the riches within. Here Brutalist treatment of cement and aggregate surface textures, and lavish customized furniture and carpets, made for surprisingly comfortable surroundings. Ever since, in the sturdiest of Oberlin traditions, annual throngs of dedicated students have made Mudd's color-coded interior their home away from home.

ART MUSEUM
New Wing
North Main

Designing additions to the chaste art museums of an earlier era has challenged the ingenuity and reputation of many prominent contemporary architects. "Like drawing a mustache on a Madonna" was Robert Venturi's phrase for it. Venturi & Rauch's 1976 addition to Cass Gilbert's Allen Art Building was named for museum benefactor Ruth Coates Roush. It showed how far the building art had travelled since Gilbert's Beaux Arts memorial of 1917, and art professor Clarence Ward's faithful rear extension of 1938. For some local observers the latest addition went too far—the most exasperating entry yet in the architectural road show surrounding Tappan Square. For others it brought a wry message about the state of the art—a complex in-joke without laughter. For Venturi's friendly critics it did no harm to his standing as postmodern architecture's most refreshing innovator.

The building's interiors are its least controversial aspect. The big bright Ellen Johnson Gallery for modern art, the industrial work space set back alongside, and the beige Clarence Ward Library above that are all sharply defined and segmented from each other and the older building. This makes the trip from library to galleries and classrooms a puzzler, especially in winter. Along the way, though, is Venturi's most disarming ornamental flourish, a stout wood-panelled Ionic column announcing the transition from new to old.

Out in front, as viewed from Main Street, a candid absence of transition in the roof lines and in the seam between Gilbert's palace and Venturi's checkerboard keeps the task of relating old and new forever lively. The red sandstone slabs in the checkerboard were taken from the same quarry used for Gilbert's building. But the quarry was quarried out, and the streaks in the slabs give their walls an oddly soiled look.

One cannot doubt the calculated declaration of discord in all this. "I am for messy vitality over unity," Venturi wrote in *Complexity and Contradiction in Architecture*, the manifesto for postmodern restlessness, a decade before his Oberlin statement went up. "I include the nonsequitor and proclaim the duality." Many veteran visitors still wonder what their next response to his proclamation will be.

**ORIGINAL
SCHOOLHOUSE**
Conservatory
Parking Lot

Oberlin's oldest building, the only one known
to survive from the colony's first decade, is
also its most mobile, having occupied four different locations since it was built in 1837. Restoration to something like its original appearance was mainly the work of businessman
Clifford Barden. He saved the building from
demolition in 1958, and with the help of many
community friends recreated Oberlin's Original Schoolhouse, now painted red.

In January 1835 the Oberlin Society, the
town's first government, appointed a committee of three prominent colonists, Nathan

Fletcher, William Hosford, and Brewster Pelton, to "consider the subject of building a school house." Fifteen months later the society authorized raising $200 for a wood frame building 20 by 24 feet, one story high, with a stone foundation. It went up near the corner of North Main and Lorain Streets, on the site of the present annex to First Church. It was too small for the local school population from the outset, and in 1851 a larger public school was built on college land just north of the present King Building. That school in turn was succeeded by the big new Union School House (Westervelt Hall) on South Main Street in 1874.

Meanwhile, the original schoolhouse had made its first migration, down Main Street to a site next to the present police station. Elizur Leonard had bought it, and turned it into a home for his sister. Later it served as a tailor shop, and after that as a home again, with additions front and rear.

When the city prepared to remove it as an eyesore in 1958, Cliff Barden launched his campaign for restoration. This required its next journey, to the hill overlooking Plum Creek on East Vine Street, perhaps the best location it ever enjoyed.

In 1968 the Oberlin Historical and Improvement Organization decided on yet another move to relocate the schoolhouse next to the Shurtleff-Monroe House south of the new Conservatory of Music. Tucked in along the conservatory parking lot, as part of a small historic strip development, the Little Red Schoolhouse is now an O.H.I.O. museum, filled with varied relics of nineteenth-century public education. It serves as a trim reminder of Oberlin's original simplicity, and the perils of preservation.

**FIRST CHURCH
Corner of Lorain
and Main**

Off to one side of Tappan Square, facing east, stands the grand old orange brick meetinghouse, Oberlin's First Church, once the moral center of a mission to spread perfection through the new American West. First Church was built from plans by Richard Bond, a prominent New England architect whom Charles G. Finney met while recruiting faculty in Boston. (The plans survive in the Oberlin College Archives.) The structure that went up in 1842–44 was actually a mix of Bond's specifications, Finney's dreams, and the will of the congregation, expressed by majority rule. Finney wanted an interior with circular seating, similar both to the arrangement in the New York City church from which he came to Oberlin in 1835 and to the revival tent he used on Tappan Square during his first years here. His dream survives only in the curve of the balcony, though according to reliable tradition he placed the pulpit to take full advantage of his strong voice and piercing eyes.

Building the church was a massive community effort, directed by Deacon Thomas P. Turner, a Vermont-born craftsman. Most of the locally fired bricks came from Pringle Hamilton's farm just south of town. Huge whitewood roof beams, 12 inches square and 75 feet long, spanned the brick walls, and pine rafters and shingles (which blew off in a storm in 1871) enclosed the meetinghouse. The tower, taken from an Asher Benjamin pattern book, was added in 1845.

58

Finney served for 37 years as pastor to the congregation, which by 1860 was the largest in the United States, rivalled only by Henry Ward Beecher's Plymouth Church in Brooklyn. Meanwhile, beginning in 1852 with a visit to Oberlin by John P. Hale, Free-Soil candidate for president, the house opened for political and secular meetings. Over the next half-century, such eminent Americans as Ralph Waldo Emerson, Frederick Douglass, Carl Schurz, Horace Greeley, Henry George, Mark Twain, Booker T. Washington, and Woodrow Wilson spoke here.

Although the auxiliary buildings north of the church have changed and expanded steadily over the years (the most recent addition going up in 1965), the outlines of the meetinghouse itself remain virtually intact. Remodellings occurred in 1882 when stained-glass windows were installed—to be replaced in 1927 by clear bubbly glass; in 1892 when 12 thick Doric columns supporting the balcony gave way to the present iron posts; in 1908 when more comfortable seating arrived; in 1927 when the pulpit and organ loft were redesigned; and in 1983 when a new ceiling went in. First Church is on the National Register.

Robert Fletcher noted years ago that "the voice of Oberlin in its youth still echoes from the walls of the old Meeting House. . . . It is not a voice of consolation but a voice of alarm. It cries out in indignant anger against all tyrants and all forms of slavery." Listen.

BARDWELL HOUSE
181 East Lorain

This little Greek Revival cottage, dating from 1846, merits community attention both on historical and architectural grounds. It is a rare example of a place for which good evidence exists of its use for harboring fugitive slaves. Its survival over the past century has been a near thing.

The front porch and picture window, twentieth-century additions, obscure the nice lines of its pediment and side-lighted doorway. It was built on the northeast corner of East Lorain and Park (then Water) for Rev. John Payne Bardwell and his wife Cornelia, whose careers embodied much of what the early Oberlin was about.

Upstate New Yorkers by birth, the Bardwells came to Oberlin in 1838. Both studied at the college through the early 1840s. John Bardwell was ordained as a Congregational minister in 1843 and became the agent for missionary efforts among the Chippewa Indians of Minnesota. He spent much time in the 1850s travelling and raising money for that cause. Meanwhile Cornelia Bardwell raised children and kept student boarders at their Oberlin home.

Her 1894 obituary tells of her hiding black fugitives in her attic during antebellum days. This account lends special interest to the structural arrangements under the eaves of the house, where sliding panels behind closet walls opened into wide dark passageways. The evidence is not clinching, but written and physical details combine with the Bardwells' character to make a credible tale—firmer than most one hears about Oberlin's underground rail network.

After the Civil War, John Bardwell went south to organize schools for black freedmen. In the spring of 1866 he was seized and beaten by a former slave owner, backed by a white mob, in Grenada, Mississippi. Returning to his work among the Chippewa, he died at Red Lake, Minnesota in 1871.

After his widow's death 23 years later, the Bardwell home stood empty for years. Neighborhood children played in its legendary secret spaces and called it a haunted house. In the early 1920s it was moved to its present location to make way for a corner grocery (now a coin laundry). Renovated for a rental property in 1981, it still awaits full restoration.

DR. JOHNSON HOUSE
49 East College

Long known as Stofan's Studio, where thousands of college students and townspeople went to sit for Andy Stofan's camera, this plain, old frame building rates notice for its longevity on a busy site. Built in 1846, it is the last of the wooden structures that made up Oberlin's first generation of downtown buildings. Most of the others disappeared in fire long ago, replaced by the brick blocks of the post-Civil War era.

For over four decades the house was the home and office of Dr. Homer Johnson, an upstate New Yorker who arrived in 1846 and practiced medicine till his death in 1890—the longest tenure of any nineteenth-century Oberlin physician. He was remembered by surviving patients for the generous drug doses he liked to prescribe.

Converted to commercial use in the 1940s, the building—despite its big display window and aluminum siding—retains the thrifty look of the early village.

WACK-DIETZ HOUSE
43 East Vine

The main section of this frame house, built in 1847, derives from the Greek Revival, as indicated by the returns at the eaves of the gable facing the street. The west wing, with its Italianate bay, is a later addition.

Chauncey Wack, Oberlin's nineteenth-century anti-hero, lived here. A native of Bennington, Vermont, Wack arrived in the village at age 24 in 1840. Over the next half-century, whatever Oberlin cherished, Wack normally opposed. For a long time he ran a rather disreputable hotel on the east side of South Main Street near the railroad depot. Among his overnight guests were the slave catchers who provoked the Wellington Rescue of 1858, a successful Oberlin effort to save fugitive John Price from being returned to slavery by way of Wellington, ten miles to the south. At the trial of the rescuers for violating the Fugitive Slave Law of 1850, Wack was a star witness for the prosecution.

Another boarder at his hotel in those days was Stephen Dorsey, a mobile young man from Vermont who married Wack's daughter Helen in 1865. Dorsey went on to achieve wealth and notoriety as a spectacularly corrupt U.S. senator from Arkansas in the 1870s. It was during Dorsey's service in Washington that Wack retired from the hotel business and moved into this house with daughter Helen. Meanwhile he had emerged as Oberlin's staunchest Democrat and was in the habit of hovering about the polls on election day to challenge blacks who

63

tried to vote. Despite an overwhelming local Republican majority, he served a term or two on the village council, and when Grover Cleveland became president in 1885, Oberlin's 126 Democrats unanimously voted to make Wack the local postmaster. To their dismay, Cleveland chose another man.

A few years after Wack's death in 1900, the house became the home of the Dietz family, which moved from New York City when Father Peter Dietz, a prominent "labor priest," took charge of Oberlin's fledgling Catholic parish. An advanced spokesman of Catholic trade unionist thought, Father Dietz remained in Oberlin from 1906 to 1912 when he left for Milwaukee and a wider field. His parents and sisters stayed on in their Oberlin home, a place of complex local memories.

**BURRELL-KING
HOUSE
317 East College**

This house has always stood apart in a class by itself. It was built in 1852 some distance from its neighbors as a sort of town seat for Jabez Lyman Burrell, who raised fine beef cattle on the surrounding acres. A native of western Massachusetts, a disciple of John Jay Shipherd, and a charter member of the college board of trustees, Deacon Burrell enjoyed substantial wealth and influence. He was an active anti-slavery man, and in 1868 he gave $10,000 for a freedmen's school in Selma, Alabama. Later he deeded valuable coal fields in Illinois to the college. In 1882 he added the gift of his house and land on East College Street. The college in turn sold the house four years later to young Henry Churchill King, who became Oberlin's president in 1902.

In Burrell's time the house was a brick cube in the Greek Revival mode, with a large extension to the rear added some time after the original construction. The attic rafters are still held in place by mortise-and-tenon joints locked with wooden pegs. The King family added the elegant porches and porte cochere, and modernized the interior, giving the place a neo-Georgian cast. It made a splendid center for the official social life of the college during King's long presidency from 1902 to 1927.

In 1974 the house was acquired by the Nordson Foundation, which built the day care center behind it. The house is on the National Register.

**McWADE HOUSE
117 South Main**

This sturdy house has weathered a lot of use,
but clings to distinction in its massive Greek
Revival doorway. James McWade, a prosperous
blacksmith, built it in 1852. A native of Vermont, McWade was one of the many skilled
craftsmen who clustered their shops on South
Main Street in Oberlin's early decades. His
Plum Creek smithy, located on the southeast
corner of Main and Vine (then Mill), was a
busy place in the 1850s. Over the next decade
James and Mary McWade put three children
through Oberlin College.

Later on, in the 1890s, their home was converted into a boardinghouse, a function it
served well into the twentieth century. Along
with its neighbors it was threatened by the
rash of commercial strip development which
broke out on South Main in the 1960s. Standing high on its old stone foundation, it has the
look of a beleaguered veteran.

HALL HOUSE
64 East College

The history of the Hall House is a blend of human achievement and architectural decline. Once known as the choicest dwelling in the village, and later the scene of happy events for college and town, it has become a rather forlorn casualty of careless maintenance.

Built in 1853 by Anson Morris, a Connecticut-born master carpenter who worked on many of the college's early buildings, it was originally a square red brick mansion of symmetrical Italianate design. Fancy double brackets once graced the eaves of roof and cupola, and massive chimneys flanked the cupola on either side. An elegant flat-roofed, columned porch shaded the first-floor French windows across the entire southern face.

In 1873 the house was bought by Rev. Heman B. Hall, an Oberlin graduate who had returned to educate his children. Hall's youngest son, Charles Martin, was a precocious lad who whiled away his hours at experiments around the house, once setting fire to the cupola. By the time he entered the college to study chemistry under Professor Frank Jewett, Charles had set up a laboratory in the family woodshed joined to the rear of the house. Here in the winter of 1886, encouraged by Jewett and assisted by sister Julia, he discovered the electrolytic process for producing aluminum—the basis of an industry and fortune from which the college prospered wonderfully after his death in 1914. Hall Auditorium and the college arboretum are

67

the most visible local monuments to his generosity.

In 1928 a plaque was applied to the house to commemorate Hall's feats. Meanwhile the "immortal woodshed" disappeared in an expansion of the house to the rear; the front porch gave way to an awkward substitute; the chimneys came down; and the brackets were stripped from the eaves. The interior was finally converted to faculty apartments. In 1980 the college removed the white spray paint it had earlier applied to the brick exterior, but further restoration remains stalled.

DASCOMB HOUSE
227 South Professor

This house is Oberlin's finest relic of the Gothic Revival, which captivated American architectural taste in the 20 years before the Civil War. Considered by some to smack of aristocratic mannerism (High Church Episcopalians were among its principal sponsors), the Gothic fashion was not widely favored in earnest Oberlin.

James Dascomb was no man to flinch before the local bias. He was a charter member of the Oberlin faculty, having arrived from New England in 1834 to teach chemistry and biology. He was also the town's first doctor. Skeptical of early village reform enthusiasms, Dascomb was, in the words of one contemporary, a "conservative force in the midst of the fervid and plastic mass at Oberlin." His wife Marianne headed the female department of the college from 1852 to 1870 and helped organize local female opposition to woman suffrage.

Their house, built in 1853-54, exhibits many of the features popularized in the work of Alexander Jackson Davis, a leading promoter of the Gothic Revival—cruciform ground plan, steeply pitched roof line, prominent front gable, bold brick chimneys. Though it is finished in careful detail—note the lancet window with its horseshoe hood mold in the front gable—the character of the house relies more on strength of form and outline than on applied decoration.

Originally it stood on the brow overlooking Plum Creek, on the present site of Johnson

69

House. From this proud bastion Dr. and Mrs. Dascomb held out against a respectful but changing world for over 25 years. When the house caught fire in a lightning storm in 1863 the stout frame held, and they were able to restore their home exactly as before. After it was moved across the street following Dascomb's death in 1880, dormer windows were added to the rear extension and a new front porch was installed. The house has been sympathetically preserved by Warren and Adele Taylor, its owners since 1939.

DANFORTH COTTAGE
228 Oak

This tidy, well-proportioned little cottage, dating from 1854, is actually some 23 years older than Oak Street itself, which was not opened until 1877. The house stood originally on West College, in the present space between Rice Hall and Dascomb Hall. It was built for Cornelia Danforth on land bought from the college on the condition (common in those days) that she employ students in manual labor.

In 1877 the town photographer Henry Platt arranged to have the house lifted from the West College lot and moved to Oak Street to make way for his new, larger dwelling. In the frugal village economy of the 1870s, the moving of wooden houses to nearby side streets was a frequent event, made easier by cheap labor, the flexibility of wood, and the lack of plumbing and electrical connections. This nineteenth-century version of the mobile home was a national phenomenon and drew much comment from European visitors, who laid it to the restlessness of a migrant, pioneering people. In the case of the Danforth cottage, the habit preserved a nice example of pre–Civil War simplicity. The little lie-on-stomach windows under the eaves, which ventilated attic crawl space, were a comely feature of domestic architecture in the 1850s.

S. G. WRIGHT HOUSE
197 West Lorain

Somewhere behind its many latter-day additions is the fabric of the house built on this corner in 1854. Eight years later it became the home of Sela G. Wright and his wife and daughters.

One of Oberlin's busiest Christian missionaries, Wright was not in town much until his last years. An upstate New Yorker who studied in the college's preparatory department as a young man, he joined the Oberlin mission to the Chippewa in Red Lake, Minnesota in 1843. He returned to Oberlin in 1846 to marry Emiline Farnsworth, who trekked back with him to the Minnesota wilderness and bore two daughters there. When the Red Lake mission collapsed in 1859, the Wrights moved to Oberlin to educate their children. During the Civil War, Wright swung his energies to helping blacks freed by the Union army in the South. Across the postwar decades he spent long stretches in Minnesota doggedly preaching the faith among the Indians. He finally retired from the field in 1889 and died in Oberlin at age 89 in 1905. His wife Emiline survived him till 1917. A daughter born at the Red Lake mission back in 1850 lived on here into the 1930s.

Young Henry Churchill King roomed at the Wright home during his undergraduate days at Oberlin. The college bought the house in 1963 and converted it to faculty housing.

72

EVANS HOUSE
33 East Vine

Oberlin's special reputation among nineteenth-century Ohio villages echoes in the history of this house. Wilson Bruce Evans, a North Carolina cabinetmaker, came to town with his wife Sarah Jane in 1854. They were among the many "free persons of color" who migrated to Oberlin before the Civil War. They quickly linked into the family network, including the Langstons, Learys, Copelands, Walls, and Scotts, which made up the leadership of the local black community in antebellum years.

Evans built his hip-roofed brick house on East Vine (then Mill) Street in 1856. Fierce talk must have crackled through its rooms over the next few years. In 1858 Evans and his brother Henry (along with Charles Langston, John Copeland, John Scott, and Orindatus Wall) joined in the Wellington Rescue of the fugitive slave John Price. Evans's brother-in-law was Lewis Sheridan Leary, the Carolina-born harness maker who joined John Copeland in John Brown's raid on Harpers Ferry in 1859. On the 113th anniversary of that raid, in 1972, the old monument to Brown's Oberlin allies was dedicated at its new site across the street from the Evans home.

At age 40 Wilson Evans enlisted in the Union army during the last year of the Civil War. He and his wife lived on in their Vine Street home till 1898. Two of their daughters attended Oberlin College in the 1880s. A granddaughter, Dorothy Inborden Miller, a Fisk University

73

graduate who spent 23 years as an educator in the Washington, D.C. school system, was instrumental in preserving the family history as well as the house. It looks much as it did when first built, aside from the addition of the front porch in 1927. The house was placed on the National Register in 1980.

LANGSTON HOUSE
207 East College

John Mercer Langston, the famous black abolitionist and civil rights leader, lived here from 1856 to 1871. Born in bondage on a Virginia plantation, the son of a white master and a slave mother, Langston was freed when his father died, and sent north to be educated. He graduated from Oberlin in 1849, read law with an antislavery judge in Elyria, and became the first black lawyer to practice in Ohio.

He proudly recalled in his autobiography that he was also the first colored homeowner on East College, the most fashionable street in town. Shortly after moving into this newly built house, Langston emerged as the acknowledged leader of the local black community, and won far-reaching prominence in abolitionist circles. On the night in January 1863 when news arrived in Oberlin of the Emancipation Proclamation, Langston read it to a packed crowd in the college chapel, and amid rockets, bonfires, and rifle salutes, black townsmen marched up East College to Langston's home to honor the event.

Langston left Oberlin after the war to work with the Freedmen's Bureau. He later joined the faculty of Howard University's law school. President Hayes named him minister to Haiti in the late 1870s, and a decade later he served a term in Congress as a Virginia Republican. He died in Washington in 1897.

Langston's home was well cared for by subsequent owners over the years, and was placed on the National Register in 1975. In 1983, Oberlin's middle school on North Main was named for him.

JOHNSON HOUSE
240 East College

This comfortable, well-landscaped house adds to the quiet dignity of Oberlin's main nineteenth-century residential thoroughfare. It is one of several homes whose early history was tied to the fortunes of the Johnson family, the town's most prosperous clan in the Gilded Age. The family patriarch, banker I. M. Johnson, made a gift of this site to his daughter-in-law Rebecca in 1868. While the records are unclear, it seems that the house standing on the lot at that time was built in 1857. A substantial addition was apparently made in 1870. Here Rebecca and Albert H. Johnson raised their family while Albert watched over his investments in coal gas and railroads. By 1884 these had flourished well enough for him to commission the fancy new Johnson mansion on South Professor Street. Thereafter yet another member of the Johnson clan moved into the East College house.

Five decades later, in 1939, novelist Louis Bromfield made this house his home for a year in between a long sojourn in Europe and his later career in scientific agriculture at Malabar Farm near Mansfield, Ohio. Bromfield spent the year campaigning vigorously for American entry into World War II. In 1959 Barry and Barbara McGill bought the house and have lived here longer than anyone else.

**MONROE-BOSWORTH
HOUSE
78 South Professor**

James Monroe, a Connecticut-born abolitionist who graduated from Oberlin in 1844, remained a leading citizen of the village for the next half-century. He built this house in 1857 and lived here in the busy pre-Civil War years while teaching rhetoric at the college, serving in the state legislature, helping to launch the Republican party, and sheltering fugitive slaves. He bought the land for his house from the college on provision that he employ students in manual labor in ratio with the acreage of his property—a common arrangement in the 1850s.

Monroe sold his home in 1862 when he left for Rio de Janeiro to serve as U.S. consul during the Civil War. (Upon his return to Oberlin after the war he purchased from Gen. Giles Shurtleff the brick house which has become known as "the Monroe House.") From the turn of the century until 1956 the old frame house on South Professor Street was owned by Bosworths—first Edward Increase Bosworth, Bible professor and dean of the theology school, then his son Edward Franklin Bosworth, dean of men at the college. More recently it has served as faculty rental housing. It is a good example of the vernacular "plain style" characteristic of mid-nineteenth-century Oberlin.

WILLIAMS HOUSE
51 North Cedar

The Greek Revival farmhouse—two wings
flanking a main block with columned portico—
was one of America's most popular domestic
adaptations of the Greek temple form, and can
still be seen gracing the landscape from New
England through the South and Middle West.
Oberlin's only example of the type is predict-
ably modest in scale and spartan in detail.
Though lacking the fine ornament of more
costly versions, it approximates the symmetry
of plan so valued by friends of the classical
forms. It was built for grocer David Williams
shortly before the Civil War, and later housed
the Lyon family, which lived here from 1887
until the 1940s. In 1965 the house was acquired by the college, which—anticipating
westward expansion of the campus—bought
up as many houses along North Cedar Street
as possible.

GREEK COTTAGE
174 East College

This attractive old house dates from the late 1850s, when East College Street began to fill fast with new homes. Although the record is unclear, the house was probably built by William Worden, a master carpenter from Connecticut who sold it to Julia Hugus in 1864. Mrs. Hugus's daughter, who lived here while attending the college during the Civil War, recalled a half-century later that the house was "nearly new" when her mother bought it. Charles Metcalf, mayor of Oberlin in the 1880s, owned the place from 1885 to 1894, when it became the home of Rev. D. L. Leonard and family. Leonard published an excellent one-volume history of Oberlin College in 1898. His son, Dr. Fred Leonard, who lived here till 1922, was a professor of physical education at the college, and the man chiefly responsible for planning Warner Gymnasium with its architect.

The Leonard home is Oberlin's most unusual survival from the Greek Revival, which flourished in northern Ohio well past 1850. Its arrangements, especially its porches, reflect an effort to domesticate the classic stone forms of temple architecture for the comfort and convenience of a wooden cottage. This was easier said than done, and Greek motifs died out in the fresh wave of home building which followed the Civil War.

CHRIST CHURCH
162 South Main

The building of Christ Church marked the arrival of religious pluralism in Oberlin. With First Church it is one of the rare institutional structures to survive from the pre-Civil War era. Episcopalians began to hold meetings in Oberlin as early as 1852. Three years later a parish was formally organized with help from Rev. Francis Granger of St. Andrews, Elyria. Work on a place of worship, slowed by scarce funds, was completed in 1859. Granger secured plans from Frank Wills, an English-born architect who had come to New York City via Canada a decade before.

Wills was an important missionary for the spread of the Gothic Revival in America, and Episcopal churches were a superb agency for the cause. Episcopalians, like their Anglican counterparts, habitually associated Christianity with the Gothic tradition and mistrusted the pagan aura of Greek and Roman architecture which had dominated popular taste in the United States since the American Revolution.

81

Wills's design for Oberlin adapted Gothic complexity to the needs of a struggling village parish. Exterior brickwork was used with economy and candor to articulate the main structural arrangements. The round arches of the windows and vestibule (the latter added in 1867) as well as the barrel vaulting of the interior strike a Romanesque note, enforcing a mood of sturdy modesty about the church.

Hard times hit Oberlin Episcopalians in the 1880s when for years they went without a rector or regular services, and in the 1970s when the parish survived a stormy quarrel over the ordination of women as priests.

The windows of the church date from the twentieth century. On the south wall of the nave is a window created in 1901 by artist Kenyon Cox and dedicated to his father Jacob Dolson Cox, an Oberlin graduate who served as a Union army general, governor of Ohio, and cabinet member to Ulysses Grant in the 1860s. The other windows, including the rose window in the east front, were designed by Margaret Kennedy, an artist in the parish, and installed between 1955 and 1960.

Christ Church is on the National Register.

GODLEY HOUSE
97 East College

Although it has been remodelled, resurfaced, and otherwise modernized over the decades, this bright cottage remains one of the small gems of early village architecture. Its Greek Revival doorway, with vernacular detail characteristic of the Western Reserve, is among the finest in town. The doorway combines with the lacy gingerbread bargeboard of the front gable to mark a transition from classical to Gothic taste which set in across the 1850s as carpenters and clients thumbed their pattern books. In this case the resulting eclecticism is a fetching example of what one historian has called "the architecture of choice."

It was built either in 1853 or 1859 (the records are cryptic on the point) by Joseph Godley. Godley was an enterprising young Scotsman who came to Oberlin by way of Troy, New York. He studied on and off at the college from 1845 to 1851, and ran a tailor shop in his first-floor room in Tappan Hall to meet expenses. Then he set up as a merchant tailor on South Main Street. Soon after the Civil War he sold the house at 97 East College and moved into a new home next door to the east. Sometime in the late 1870s he moved to Kansas, where he died in 1885.

In a neighborhood of relatively high turnover, the house enjoyed loyal owners after that. The

Mumford family lived here from the 1890s to 1939, followed by Frank and Agnes Felkner for 35 more years.

ALLENCROFT
134 South Professor

Allencroft has been rich with special memories for every generation of Oberlinians since it was built. An asymmetrical, receding stack of brick cubes, it stands as a kind of local prototype for the Italianate style which served to compromise the rivalry between Greek and Gothic beginning in the 1860s. (The compromise had set in on the eastern seaboard 15 years earlier.) Ralph Plumb, a hero of the Wellington Rescue, had the house built in 1861. Plumb and his brother Samuel were upstate New York abolitionists who came to Oberlin in 1855 and promptly joined the village elite. A restless lawyer-politician with an eye for the main chance, Plumb joined the Quartermaster Corps of the Union army the year his house went up. Soon after the war he left Oberlin with his brother for Streator, Illinois to make his fortune in coal mine speculation and become a Republican congressman.

Dr. Dudley Allen, a popular and cultivated physician, took possession of the house in 1865. Neighbors remarked on the Allen family's fondness for collecting objects of art and beauty, not a common village trait. A son, Dudley Peter Allen, graduated from the college in 1875 and later became an important Cleveland surgeon. Shortly after his death in 1915, gifts to the college from his widow made possible Allen Art Building (1917) and Allen Memorial Hospital (1925). Meanwhile the family home had passed to the college in 1899, and begun its long career as a dormitory, first for academy children, later for conservatory and college women. Recently it has served as Russian House.

The house underwent several changes over the years. Dr. Allen added bay windows and more space to the rear in 1872. The college enlarged the rear again in 1913, periodically remodelled the interior, and narrowed the front porch in 1952. Stripped of the flourishing trumpet vines which once climbed over its porches, balconies, and cornices, Allencroft in its dark, flat-roofed containment seems reminiscent of the urban brownstone mood of American cities in the Civil War era.

The main section of this elegant Italianate house is a cube of warm red brick with low-pitched hip roof and wide, bracketed eaves. Its construction was reported in the village paper in 1862. The gable-roofed section to the rear possibly antedates the main structure.

The house was built for George Stevens, the town postmaster whose wife Orpha attended the college in 1841–42. Stevens bought his lot from Professor Henry Peck, whose trim Gothic cottage once stood just to the west on the present site of Eastwood School. In 1867 Stevens moved to Iowa after selling his home to Zoraster Culver, a retired merchant from upstate New York. In 1881 the house was bought by H. Delos Wood, and remained in Wood family hands for over 90 years thereafter. The only major change in its external appearance occurred in 1913, when new porches on front and sides replaced the originals.

HALLAUER HOUSE
131 Groveland

Dozens of Oberlin's early skilled craftsmen—white, black, and mulatto, to use the federal census terms—lived in small homes along the streets of the town's southeast quadrant, and some of the most interesting domestic architecture dating from its early decades was clustered here.

Although many of these houses have been torn down or greatly altered over the years, several survive in something close to their original appearance. One example is the sturdy red brick cottage built in 1862 by Jacob Hallauer, the founder of Oberlin's Hallauer family. Its lintels, sills, and brickwork reflect a sure and careful hand at work. It may have been the first house on Groveland, which was opened up to Main Street the following year.

Jacob Hallauer was born in Switzerland in 1816 and was apprenticed as a stone cutter, a trade he practiced in many Swiss towns before sailing for New York in 1848. Three years later he returned to Europe, gathered his big family for the transatlantic migration, and settled in northern Ohio. The family remained on Groveland through the 1870s. Five generations of Jacob Hallauer's descendants have lived in Oberlin since.

This handsome place is a happy example of the charm that could result from eclectic home improvement. Its earliest version, dating from the late 1850s, was a plain, oblong, frame farmhouse. In 1862 the owner, John Clark, enlarged and refurbished it. The transformation inspired the local newspaper to pronounce it "one of the finest places in town." Clark's changes no doubt included most of the features which lend an Italianate air—the twin bays flanking an elegant flat-roofed porch entry, the bracketed eaves (particularly fine at the gable ends), and the balustraded twin chimneys creating a cupola effect at the center of the roof ridge.

In the mid-1880s the house became the home of Judge John Steele, the main man in the public life of the village in the late nineteenth century. Steele was the son of Dr. Alexander Steele, a physician who arrived in town in 1836. The son came home from the Civil War bearing a splendid record and promptly won election as a probate judge. He then left the country for several years to pursue railroading in Canada and South America. On his return to Oberlin he moved in with the Clarks, whose daughter he had married. Steele soon became the Republican leader of the town, twice serving as postmaster. He was a prime mover in the building of the village waterworks on Morgan Street and the county orphans' home on East College. A hearty, gregarious man, given to occasional profanity and regular cigars,

Judge Steele was a refreshing first citizen for sober Oberlin.

Later owners made substantial additions to the rear of the house, the most important coming in 1913. Robert and Margaret Kilmer have lived here since 1956.

**BAILEY-GAGER
HOUSE
145 West Lorain**

This picturesque home, built in 1862 for a
young Massachusetts-born shoemaker named
William Bailey, sheltered Bailey and his wife
and nine children for a decade before he left for
Cleveland in 1873. Twelve years later the
Gager family from Norwalk moved in, and one
or more of the Gagers lived here through the
next 60 years. After the college bought the
house in 1948, it became the home of librarian
Dorothy Daub.

It is a nice study in the cumulative home improvement widely practiced among nineteenth-
century villagers. The exact history of its various side and rear additions remains in the
realm of speculation. Most intriguing are the
geometrically patterned bargeboards over the
north and east gables and the matching front
and side porches. These decorative features
were clearly a later addition (in a style once
called "Eastlake") to what was originally a
pretty plain brick house. In fact the bargeboard
on the front gable obscures a small round-
headed window in the apex of the gable. Taste
trends suggest that the porches and bargeboards were added in the late 1880s, when
Eastlake gingerbread was much in vogue. Once
painted to accentuate their intricacy, they have
been more recently covered with white paint,
as have the stone windowsills and lintels.

Beginning with the construction of Men's
Building (now Wilder Hall) next door in 1910,
the expanding college began to change the

neighborhood. The house came close to demolition for a parking lot when Mudd Learning Center went up in the early 1970s. But preservation instincts surfaced to save it for a while longer.

GOSS-WAGER HOUSE
292 West College

Shaded by its ancient gnarled pines, this old brick house stands at what was once the western end of West College Street. Roswell Stevens, a village carpenter, built it in 1862 on land purchased from the college and sold it to Charles Goss in 1865. Goss's wife Abigail, who had been converted by Charles G. Finney at age 14, was a successful milliner. For 20 years after the Civil War she ran the smartest dress shop in town. "Mrs. Goss is constantly on the market," the local paper observed in 1870, "and everything that is new and stylish is always purchased for her customers." She died one day in March 1885 from internal injuries suffered while lifting a hod of coal to fill her stove.

At the turn of the century Professor Charles H. A. Wager bought the house and lived here through his long (1900–1934) and distinguished career as a teacher of English literature at the college. Few professors have left as compelling memories among their students as Charles Wager. Novelist Thornton Wilder remembered him as "the greatest class lecturer I have ever heard." A wing of North Hall on the college campus is named in Wager's honor.

93

**WESTWOOD
CEMETERY
Morgan**

The landscaped cemetery was a nineteenth-century American invention. When the first of them, Mt. Auburn cemetery in Cambridge, Massachusetts, was opened in 1831, it soon became a popular place for family picnics and weekend strolls. Cemeteries were discovered to be an urban space for the living as well as the dead. Historians of landscape architecture believe that this helped inspire growing support for urban public parks.

Oberlin's Westwood Cemetery was an early example of the new-style burying ground. The original village graveyard had been located above Plum Creek along Morgan between Main and Professor streets. By the 1860s it was crowded and unsightly. Shortly after the Civil War broke out, a search began for more suitable space to honor the dead. A large tract of open fields, orchard land, and uncleared forest west of town was finally selected. An experienced designer, H. B. Allen, provided plans for a cemetery of curving lanes and gentle, tree-shadowed slopes in the romantic English landscape tradition popularized in this country by Andrew Jackson Downing.

Westwood was formally opened in 1864. Early celebrations of Memorial Day in the 1870s included a march of villagers through town to the cemetery to decorate the graves of soldiers and relatives with flowers. As a guard against more furtive visits, many coffins were equipped with "torpedoes" to discourage grave robbers, according to a newspaper note of August 1890.

A slow walk through Westwood remains among the more pleasant ways to reconstruct the lives of Oberlin's majority, famous and obscure.

Over long decades the iron horse was a central
fact about America, impressing its rhythms,
sights, and sounds on daily life in elemental
ways now all but forgotten—the warning
whistle's wail, the measured thunder of approach, the stranger's face at the spattered
window. Trains compressed distance, broke
down community isolation, and imposed a semi-
public style on the experience of travel. The
depot, main portal to the town for students,
parents, businessmen, and travellers of all
kinds, was a meeting place alive with expectation, connecting the village with the world.

Oberlin's first rail line came through in 1852.
The new depot went up a year after the Civil
War, when direct service opened to Elyria, cut-
ting travel time to the county seat from two
hours to 20 minutes. The depot's completion
was a moment of some pride in the village.
"We may reasonably expect," the local paper
declared, "that our depot will contribute
greatly to the removal of any wrong opinion as
to the beauty of the town." A well-proportioned
building with broad eaves to protect pas-
sengers from the weather, the depot housed
telegraph, ticket, and baggage offices as well as
separate gaslit waiting rooms for gentlemen
and ladies. The exterior board-and-batten walls
were painted stone gray with dark gray trim.
In the spring of 1867 station agent Lester Kinney set out 125 shade trees and 25 evergreens
in the surrounding park with its curving
gravel carriage drive. The great age of steam

transportation was underway, with half a dozen daily trains connecting Oberlin east and west.

Then the automobile came along. The railroad era ended in 1949 when Oberlin's last passenger train, nicknamed the Plug by villagers who used its 6:20 A.M. whistle for an alarm clock, made its final run by order of the Ohio Public Utilities Commission. Twenty years later the Nordson Foundation renovated the depot for use as a Headstart school. Its exterior has been faithfully preserved.

The depot is on the National Register.

**DEACON THOMPSON
HOUSE
199 West College**

The "plain style" of early Oberlin is perpetuated in the austere and uncompromising lines of this house. The large bay on the west side and the rear wing were added later to the simple, oblong frame dwelling which went up in 1866. Deacon Uriah Thompson was a rich man by village standards and could have built himself a more lavish place, but this is what he wanted.

Thompson had come to Oberlin from Vermont in 1840. A radical antislavery man, he was also strenuously opposed to liquor, secret societies, and all other forms of self-indulgence. On the strength of these credentials as well as his personal wealth, he was elected to the college board of trustees in 1850 and helped manage the college's business affairs for 40 years as a member of the prudential committee. President James Fairchild counted him among the more vigorous early patrons of the college.

In 1883 Thompson sold his corner house and moved across the street into a section of First Ladies Hall which had been moved west on College Street from its original downtown location. He boarded students in this relic, which acquired the name "Poverty Barn" before its demolition in 1896. Thompson himself died at age 86 in 1890.

Oberlin's ranking Civil War hero, Gen. Giles Shurtleff, built three substantial homes in the village during the postwar years. This is the first of them. Shortly after the war, Colonial Hall—one of the earliest college dormitories—was dismantled to make way for the erection of the Second Congregational Church (where the Conservatory of Music now stands). A choice block of residential sites, called College Place, was opened around the church, and here General Shurtleff's red brick Italianate villa went up in the summer of 1866.

James Monroe bought the house from Shurtleff in 1870 upon his return from Rio de Janeiro, where he had served as Lincoln's consular representative during the war. Monroe was Oberlin's leading antislavery politician. In 1865 he married Rev. Charles G. Finney's daughter Julia and turned down a bid from the faculty to succeed Finney as president of the college. He served five terms in Congress as a Republican across the 1870s, and after that taught history and political economy at the college. A charming and knowledgeable sage, he was among the most popular professors of his day.

Sixty-two years after the death of this much-honored man, when the construction of the new conservatory obliterated College Place, the Oberlin Historical and Improvement Organization saved Monroe's house by moving it 100 yards south to its present site. It stood boarded up and empty for 20 years, luring vandals and

breeding legends, but in the early 1980s
O.H.I.O. took steps to make it a living place
again. Its restoration was completed just in
time for Oberlin's sesquicentennial year, 1983.

KENNEY HOUSE
10 South Prospect

John T. Kenney, a prosperous farmer from Brighton, Ohio, moved to Oberlin with his wife and eight children after the Civil War and built this gabled brick Italianate home in 1867. While some of its decorative finery has disappeared, the wooden scrollwork and "seahorse" brackets have survived a long century of Oberlin weather in good condition.

Kenney's wife, Olive Wadsworth Kenney, was a Wellington girl who attended Oberlin College in the 1840s. Her father shared Oberlin's anti-slavery passions and joined in the Wellington Rescue of fugitive John Price in 1858. He stands with the rescuers in the famous photograph taken in a Cleveland jail yard after the rescue.

One of the Kenneys' daughters, Mary Editha, was the last survivor of the college class of 1875. She lived on in the family home on South Prospect for the rest of her life, save one year in middle age spent teaching at a school for mountain girls in Blowing Rock, North Carolina. She bicycled the streets of Oberlin till age 80, and died at 93 in 1943. A old photo of the Kenney house in the college archives shows her sitting in the morning sunlight at her bedroom window back in the 1870s, reading a book.

STONE HOUSE
42 North Park

This small, solid cottage is an Oberlin rarity, a house made of sandstone blocks. Despite access to nearby quarries in Amherst and Berea, and the sustained use of sandstone by the college in its late nineteenth-century architecture, stone never caught on as a domestic building material in the town. This place was built in 1867 by J. J. Hill for Uriel Hill, who ran it as a boarding house for bachelor tradesmen. The cloverleaf cutouts in the window shutters recall a later phase in its career, from 1942 to 1953, when local girl scouts used it for their rendezvous.

TEACHOUT HOUSE
169 North Pleasant

Brick mason Marvin Teachout, who arrived in Oberlin during the Civil War, brought a touch of urban cosmopolitanism to the village when he built this red brick mansard house in 1867. The mansard style was imported from France just before the war and swept the country in the postwar decade. Its elegance, order, and bulk appealed to a nation tired of war and eager for the ornaments of peace and prosperity. The fashion was especially popular in urban America, where cramped land space gave value to the extra attic rooms tucked under the steep pitch of the mansard roof. The mansard craze of the 1960s, widely favored among condominium and commercial strip developers, rolled through just a century after the first wave.

The Teachout family lived in this house until 1904. Renovated in 1963 by contractor Kenny Clark with advice from architect William B. Durand, it is the older of two surviving nineteenth-century brick mansard homes in Oberlin.

LANG HOUSE
214 West College

This house, a relaxed and cheerful variant of carpenter Gothic styling, has long been a local favorite among friends of Victorian architecture. It went up in 1870. The porch and an addition to the rear date from the early twentieth century. Once even more eyecatching in appearance than now, the house lost some years ago the crockets and finials (an unusual touch of gaiety for Oberlin) which originally graced its gables and dormers.

The house was built for Jesse Lang, an 1848 graduate of the college preparatory department who returned to town in 1868 after an early career in Wisconsin. Over the next 40 years Lang proved himself a jack of many trades—realtor, compiler of illustrated Bible books for children, and pension lawyer for Civil War veterans. This latter calling often got him into trouble with the government for filing false claims. He died in 1917 at age 92.

Since the 1920s the house has been a very popular rooming house for college students.

RICE-MOORE HOUSE
155 Elm

In 1871 college president James Fairchild had this house built (apparently as an investment) by a local carpenter named J. S. Wright, who lived in it until 1874. Then Fairchild sold it to Fenelon B. Rice, the enterprising young director of the college's new conservatory of music. Rice had come to Oberlin after several years of intensive study in piano at Leipzig, Germany. Director of the conservatory for 30 years, he was more than any other man responsible for its emergence to national renown in the late nineteenth century. His wife Helen, an accomplished singer also trained at Leipzig, taught vocal music at the conservatory. Rice Hall, now a faculty office building, is named for them.

In 1916 their Elm Street home was purchased by Professor David R. Moore, who taught European and Latin American history at the college from 1913 to 1943. The college bought the place for a dormitory in 1965 and later divided it into faculty apartments. The exterior, still reasonably intact, shows in its easy horizontal lines the broad range of domestic design possibilities inherent in the Italianate mode.

DUDLEY FARM
Route 10 (West of Town Line)

This weatherbeaten old brick mansion has been a familiar landmark to travellers entering Oberlin from the west for well over a century.

Built in 1871 for Stowell B. Dudley, it is very similar in design to the house which General Shurtleff built near the center of town five years earlier—in the distinctive line of the roof, the fenestration in the front facade, and the stone horseshoe lintels over the windows. Dudley's house differs in the absence of a cupola and in the broad wooden frieze wrapping around the house beneath the bracketed eaves.

Dudley, a native of Vermont, lived here with his English-born wife, four children, two black hired servants, and his mother-in-law. He ran a thriving dairy farm on the surrounding acres. Meanwhile, with an eye to the future, he bought up a good deal of rural property to the north of Oberlin. His investment paid off a generation later. In 1906 Dudley's son John came by a pleasant windfall of $7,500 when he sold a right-of-way across his property to a rail line connecting the steel mills of Lorain to the coal fields of West Virginia.

DURAND HOUSE
140 Elm

Elm filled quickly with new houses in the decade after the Civil War. The street was laid
out in 1868 across land previously used to pas-
ture the cows of President James Fairchild and
Professor George Allen, who were neighbors at
the eastern end of the street. (Fairchild's house
stood on the present site of the dormitory bearing his name.)

Many of the early Elm Street homes came
down in the 1960s to create a vista for South
Hall. Among the more graceful survivors is
this frame Italianate, built in 1873 for William
B. Durand, an insurance agent who long
served as town clerk. Its generous polygonal
bays and tall windows give the house a cheerful, sunny air which has been well preserved
across the decades. The Durand family lived
here for 70 years. William B. Durand, grandson
of the original owner and an architect of some
skill, helped his sister divide the 28 rooms of
the house into apartments in the early 1940s.
In its old age the place retains a look of comfortable Victorian gentility. One of its first-floor
apartments is the Oberlin home of Democratic
congressman Don Pease and his wife Jeanne.

**UNION SCHOOL
HOUSE**
South Main

Built in 1874, this rugged relic of the Gilded Age entered its second century empty and vulnerable. But in the early 1980s it made a rousing comeback as an emblem of sesquicentennial pride.

In its heyday it housed 700 school children. Its construction was a response to overcrowding in the local schools as public education took off after the Civil War. Cleveland architect Walter Blythe provided the plans, calling for a Victorian Gothic monument in red brick, trimmed with sandstone to create a polychromatic effect originally dramatized by a brightly tiled roof. John Berg, a young Bavarian immigrant stonemason, supervised construction by local craftsmen, and Lester Kinney supplied the brick from his Plum Creek kilns. The open bell tower crowning the design weakened over the decades and was taken down in 1940.

After a more modern high school (now the Langston middle school) opened on North Main in 1923, Edmund Westervelt bought the old schoolhouse and gave it to the college, which used it for classes till 1961. Then the long campaign to save it got underway.

Imposing, cavernous, and gritty, the building challenged conventional modern taste and irritated downtown commercial developers. In line with the urban renewal thinking of the early 1960s, one consultant briskly advised: "raze the present structure and . . . use the parcel for a gasoline service station." Ideas for a kinder fate, including adaptive reuse as a city hall or a combination of shops and apartments, attracted wide support but little money. In 1974 the building was placed on the National Register. But as late as 1981 the town paper called for the demolition of "that moldering eyesore."

Then contractor Kenny Clark, who had bought it in 1977, settled the debate by launching his renovation. The town sesquicentennial committee used it for a headquarters in 1983, and "Old Westervelt" began a bright if uncertain new career.

DRAKE HOUSE
237 West College

George Drake was the sort of man that early Oberlin produced in droves. He came here from New Jersey in 1838 to begin his schooling at age 20. The colony was still emerging from the woods when he arrived, and he put his skill in masonry right to work at 10 cents an hour. Converted by the preaching of Oberlin's first president, Asa Mahan, he entered the college, thrived on Graham dieting, helped build First Church, and graduated in 1843. Next he prepared for missionary work at the theological seminary and the Western Reserve medical school. He wanted to go to Africa, but apparently the prejudice in conventional missionary circles against radical Oberlin Perfectionism blunted that desire. He went to preach in Iowa instead. Two decades later he returned to Oberlin with his wife Laura (an Oberlin graduate of 1846) to educate their children.

In 1874 he put up this nicely crafted red brick house. The porches were added four years later. In 1883 Drake left town for a final stint of missionary work in the Dakota Territory. He died in Michigan in 1909.

Shortly before World War I, the Woodruff family acquired the house, and for 20 years Althea Woodruff ran one of the most attractive college rooming houses in town—"Mrs. Woody's." Then it became the home of Professor and Mrs. Herbert May. May, a noted biblical scholar, taught at Oberlin from 1934 to 1970. Five years later William and Nancy Holodnick took possession and set to work restoring the interior. They also installed the handmade leaded glass lunette at the apex of the gable facing the street.

G. F. WRIGHT HOUSE
145 Elm

This was the longtime home of the famous Oberlin geologist George Frederick Wright, who was a pioneering student of Ice Age glacial action and an important mediator in the controversy touched off by Charles Darwin's evolutionary theories. Wright graduated from Oberlin in 1859. After training for the ministry at the Oberlin theological seminary he worked up an interest in geology while filling the pulpits of several New England churches. He returned to teach at the college in 1881 and bought this house from Margaret Snyder, for whom it was built in 1875.

Wright's subsequent geological work included a survey of the terminal morain in the northern United States, a study of Alaskan glaciers, and forays across Greenland and Siberia. Meanwhile he joined the dispute over biblical accounts of human origin. Darwin's rival account disturbed Oberlinians. At a meeting on the issue in 1871, Dr. Dascomb noted the bad effect of evolutionary thought on morals and warned that "a person who reads Mr. Darwin's books is very apt to be carried right along with them unless he is on his guard." Professors John Morgan and Charles Henry Churchill, among others, added more authority to the resistance. Wright's contribution was to argue that a divinity surely shaped the ends of life, "let natural selection rough hew them as it will." To reward his wisdom the college in 1892 created for him a special professorship in the Harmony of Science and Revelation.

His Elm Street house was noted in those days for the strange rocks he brought home from his travels and piled near his front door. After his death in 1921 the place became a student rooming house, and it was purchased by the college in 1969. Its clapboards have been covered with composition shingles, its eaves clipped short, and its brackets removed. The big twin bays facing the street remain an unusual feature of Oberlin's Victorian architecture.

HART HOUSE
525 East College

The younger of two surviving brick mansard houses in Oberlin, this place was built in 1875 for 26-year-old Flavius Hart, one of Oberlin's more affluent merchants. His father, Sylvester Hart, ranked among the 20 richest men in the village in the 1860s. Flavius attended the college preparatory department in the late sixties, and a decade later was running a feed and cider mill on the land next to his house. Later he opened a small furniture factory on what is now South Park Street, with a retail outlet on South Main next to the Union School House. Like many other nineteenth-century furniture dealers he also ran a sideline in undertaking.

Hart was a Democrat, an oddity among Oberlin businessmen. When the Democrats came to power in Washington under Grover Cleveland in 1885 for the first time since the Civil War, a long search got underway for a respectable local member of the party who might serve as village postmaster. Cleveland finally named Hart in 1894. Fulfilled by four years at this post, Hart retired at age 50 to farm the land around his house until his death in 1918.

114

TOWER HOUSE
111 Forest

While Oberlin is relatively rich in examples of the Italianate variety that swept America in the mid-nineteenth century, this is the only survivor of its particular kind. The bracketed tower is its central feature, establishing a focus for the informal, slightly rambling elements of the overall design. Elsewhere brick, stone, or stucco were favored for more pretentious compositions along this line. The gently curving planes of the tower roof rising to a flat octagonal crown, the tall French windows shaded by the front porch, and the intricate symmetry in the design of the front door are noteworthy details in the Oberlin example.

The house was built in 1876 for the clothing merchant Edward P. Johnson, one of the town's famous Johnson boys, a brother of the man who built Johnson House on South Professor. As this place neared completion, a neighbor went through it and was awed by its modern conveniences: "It is all in very good style. Kitchen and pantry are full of cupboards, drawers, shelves and all that. On the west side the front parlor opens by folding door into the dining room. . . . Has very nice dressing room speaking tubes, and water tubes with force pump. Cellar magnificent." The cost of the house was even more impressive—close to $1,000.

The place acquired the name "Tower House" in the 1920s when it served as a private boardinghouse for a dozen college men.

115

COLBURN HOUSE
30 Groveland

Lyman Colburn was among the many village craftsmen who settled along Groveland in the Civil War era. An upstate New York native, he came to Oberlin with his wife Martha in 1858. The Wellington Rescue excitement gripped the town just after their arrival, and for the rest of her life Mrs. Colburn loved to read about it. For years her husband ran a planing mill on the northwest corner of South Main and Vine streets. He was an inventive carpenter and worked out many labor-saving improvements in woodworking machinery at his mill. In 1876 he built a new home on Groveland three blocks west of his earlier house. A trim, angular wood frame structure, it gains identity from the variety of machine-milled custom details: the collar-brace gable decorations, the Italianate bay-and-balcony facing the street, the elaborate round-headed, double-panelled doorway on the side porch.

Colburn died in 1905. His daughter, Cora Czarena Colburn, carried his ingenuity and enterprise into her own career. After several years of study at the Oberlin conservatory in the late 1880s, and a short stint teaching music in Crockett, Texas, she moved to Boston and plunged into the new science of home economics, just then on the brink of its early twentieth-century boom. She was soon a recognized expert in creating modern living and dining facilities for college students. In 1910 she joined the University of Chicago faculty to teach home economics, and six years later she

116

took charge of the university's food service. She specialized in designing more efficient equipment for the storage and preparation of food in big institutional kitchens. In 1923 she left Chicago to become director of the Yale University dining halls. Over the next decade she was much involved in organizing the eating arrangements for Yale's new undergraduate colleges. Long before her death in 1939, the girl from Groveland Street had established her authority in the thick of a major new growth industry.

EVANS HOUSE
172 Elm

William Evans, a Welsh mason who emigrated with his bride to the United States in 1865, made money by designing railroad bridges. He built this house in 1877. Quite traditional in appearance, it might have gone up any time after 1840. Its solid, unpretentious lines reflect a man less concerned with canons of current architectural taste than with substance, function, and comfort. Gently arched stone caps over the windows and the decorative porthole in the gable relieve the general restraint of exterior flourish.

The house passed through many owners after the Evans family, and if persistent local folk tradition may be trusted, it acquired a ghost sometime after the turn of the century. The faint, mysterious cries of a small child floating from the rear rooms of the house were originally blamed on a demented maid trying to scare the spinster sisters who lived here at the time. Sisters and maid have long since gone to their reward, but novelist Diane Vreuls and her husband, poet Stuart Friebert, testify that they have heard the strange cries more than once since moving into the house in 1967.

A. A. WRIGHT HOUSE
123 Forest

For almost a century this house was linked with two prominent Oberlin academic families, the Wrights and the Taylors. It was built for Albert Allen Wright on land originally owned by his father, William Wheeler Wright.

W. W. Wright, an early graduate of the college, helped manage the college farm during the 1840s. When the college abandoned collective farming, he bought up most of the acreage, which extended westward from his rambling frame house on South Professor. Just after the Civil War, Wright opened his nursery lands for residential development along a new street, appropriately named Forest. In 1874 he planted the picturesque rows of Scotch pine along Forest west of Cedar.

A. A. Wright, a professor of botany and geology, built the front part of this house, with its angular flaring roof line and proud decorative chimney, in 1880. Choice chestnut and walnut woodwork graced the interior. A large rear section was added to the house about a decade later. In 1905 a major renovation occurred, bringing indoor plumbing and a new front porch. Wright's boy Norman later recalled this as the point in his life when he learned from the contractor's son "certain much-used parts of the language which my mother had somehow neglected to teach me."

Professor Lloyd W. Taylor, an eminent physicist, lived here during most of his teaching career, 1924–48. He died in a mountain-climbing accident on Mt. St. Helens near Spirit Lake, Washington. His wife, Esther B. Taylor, Oberlin's last forceful temperance leader, maintained the family home until 1975.

ARNOLD HOUSE
181 Forest

Grain merchant George Arnold, who had this house built in 1880, was greatly interested in the profits of modernization. He helped patch together Oberlin's first intercity telephone exchange in 1881, having landed the Bell franchise for Lorain County. When the exchange collapsed six years later for lack of subscribers, it seemed like an object lesson in the consequences of monopoly control over the greatest invention of the day. Peering into his murky crystal ball, the village editor prophesied, "The time will probably come when it will cost little more to have a telephone than a clock."

Arnold's house was a somber expression of the Italianate style, which peaked locally in the early 1880s. What once must have been the last word in external elegance now seems very formal and severe.

For several decades in the early twentieth century the house was the family home of Professor Simon Fraser MacLennan, who taught psychology, philosophy, and comparative religion at the college from 1897 to 1933.

In 1971 architect Pamela Segal, fresh from the Georgetown ambiance of Washington, D. C., imposed a stylish renovation on the interior, opening spaces, rearranging functions, and mixing tradition with contemporary zest. It was a bright revival, but you wouldn't know it from the street.

In February 1880, James N. Wright, a prosperous timber merchant from the Keweenaw peninsula of Upper Michigan, bought a double lot on Elm Street just as his daughter Harriet prepared to enter the Oberlin conservatory. He had this impressive brick house built for his family the following summer. It marked a departure from the local architectural conventions of the day, which still ran mostly to variations on the Italianate. The broad eaves and bold timberwork about the porch carry a suggestion of Swiss chalet styling, just then coming into vogue. And the subtle figures laid into the brickwork on the front face of the house show an uncommon attention to decorative detail.

After daughter Harriet married Howard Handel Carter on a trip abroad in 1892, the Carters made this place their home. Carter had graduated from the conservatory in 1874 and taught pianoforte there from 1881 to 1923.

Dewey and Carol Ganzel bought the house in 1967. Over the years since, they have refinished the interior with period furnishings and have done much to restore the aesthetic impact of both house and grounds.

122

COMMERCIAL BLOCK
Corner of College and Main

In March 1882 the worst fire in Oberlin's history blazed through the business district, destroying nine buildings clustered near the southeast corner of the main intersection. Within three weeks rubble was being cleared for a modern commercial block on the site. Cleveland architect Walter Blythe supplied the plans. He had earlier designed two soaring Victorian Gothic structures for Oberlin— Council Hall (demolished in 1930 to make way for Cass Gilbert's Bosworth Hall) and the Union School House (later known as Westervelt, and still standing).

Blythe's block reflected several new trends in commercial architecture which came out of Chicago after that city's great fire of 1871. Hints of the future appeared week by week as the building rose from its foundations across the summer: the iron skeleton of supporting columns and crossbeams; the smooth pressed brick ("Chicago brick") of the exterior facing; the big plate-glass windows of the new store fronts. Oberlin had its first urban building.

In November 1882 the hardware store at the block's south end held its grand opening. While a cornet band played from the store's second floor gallery and an impromptu guitar troupe sang jubilee songs, a patent elevator whisked shoppers up and down from basement to storeroom. An oyster dinner for visiting reporters completed the rousing celebration.

123

For years E. J. Goodrich's bookstore clung to the space at the corner, a site it had held since 1857. In 1923 the bookstore gave way to the Oberlin Savings Bank as the central landmark of the business district. In 1972 bank president Ray Campbell supervised an extensive renovation of the entire block and introduced a handsome antique street clock to the corner scene.

GINGERBREAD HOUSE
211 North Pleasant

Oberlin could support few examples of the bizarre domestic castles favored by opulent Americans in the Gilded Age. This fetching fancy on North Pleasant suggests the opportunities for show available to people of more modest means. Nothing quite like it had been seen in town before. When it went up in the summer of 1883, the village paper primly remarked, "There is quite a contrast in the matter of ornament between the original dwellings of the people of Oberlin and some of the recent structures with their superfluity of gingerbread work."

The house was built for insurance agent E. W. Chamberlain. Its plain vertical lines are tricked out with an eye-catching variety of detail: narrow bay, porch and stoop; festooned window moldings and brackets under the eaves; and perky gables breaking the roof line. Like a contemporary Victorian parlor, the busy exterior celebrates the possibilities of applied decoration, a quaint reminder of the days before form began dutifully to follow function.

JEWETT HOUSE
73 South Professor

Frank Fanning Jewett, the famous Oberlin chemistry professor, lived here for 40 years. The house was begun for Rev. Reuben Hatch, who sold it unfinished to Jewett in 1884. Jewett belonged to a new breed of Oberlin scholars. He was a university-trained professional who had studied at Yale, Harvard, and in Germany, and taught briefly at the Imperial University in Tokyo before joining the Oberlin faculty in 1880. His expert discipline proved fruitful to many an Oberlin undergraduate, including Charles Martin Hall, who worked under Jewett's guidance in the years leading up to his discovery of the electrolytic process for making aluminum. Mrs. Jewett (Frances Gulick Jewett), the daughter of Christian missionaries, authored several books on personal and community hygiene.

The Jewett house is similar to many which went up about town in the 1880s—lean, asymmetrical, and angular, marking a transition from the Italianate to the Queen Anne style. Subtle details like the gently flared gable roof, the triangular indentation in the brickwork of the gables, and the curved window moldings, relieve a rather stern exterior. The stained-glass window lighting the stair landing on the south wall is a particular delight. In 1891 the veranda was added, in the popular stick style of the day.

The inside of the house, rich in figured oak woodwork, was kept pretty much intact by the Hubbard family which lived here for 40 years following Jewett's death in 1926. The house is now maintained by the Oberlin Historical and Improvement Organization, and was placed on the National Register in 1979.

LESLIE HOUSE
190 Elm

In the year of its construction (1884) this somber, arresting house won much comment for the advance it marked in both fashion and technology. Modelled on a reduced scale after a home in Elyria, it mixed a Gothic mood with the eclecticism of Queen Anne. The steep, hovering bulk of the slate roof lent proportion to the boxy massing below and made a unifying hood for the irregular shapes and surfaces of the gabled front facade.

The village paper pronounced the house a great success and remarked on the airy elegance of the big first-floor rooms opening off an oak-panelled main hall. Especially newsworthy was the steam furnace—one of Oberlin's first—sending warmth from the cellar through registers in every room. Central heating had arrived in town with style. As elsewhere it would ultimately transform the concept of family living space, turn the fireplace into an aesthetic luxury, and make possible the spacious, flowing room arrangements of the twentieth century.

Florence Leslie lived in her new house only five years before selling it to Calista Andrews, an Oberlin graduate who returned to town to educate her wards. Around 1911 it became the home of Rebecca Johnson, the widow of the Oberlin capitalist who built Johnson House on South Professor. More recently it has been a friendly home for student roomers.

128

The Johnson family gave Oberlin its most spectacular link with the flamboyant world of nineteenth-century capitalism. The patriarch of the clan, I. M. Johnson, was president of the first national bank of Oberlin and lived on East College Street in the big house later known as Cranford (destroyed in 1971) until he retired to the California coast in 1878. One of his sons, Edward, was a longtime village clothing merchant. Another was Albert H. Johnson, who worked as cashier in his father's bank and then as owner of the Oberlin gasworks before becoming president of the Arkansas Midland Railroad.

In the early 1880s Albert Johnson bought the old Dascomb property and several acres around it on South Professor. He then moved the Dascomb house across the street, and asked Cleveland architect George Horatio Smith to plan a suitable home for him on the rise above Plum Creek. Smith, who would co-design the Cleveland Arcade five years later, was already well known for his service to the housing needs of the Euclid Avenue elite. His Oberlin response was Johnson House, completed in 1885, the instant showpiece of the town, a domestic Peters Hall.

With Johnson House the Queen Anne enthusiasm, imported from England by way of the 1876 Philadelphia Centennial Exposition, hit Oberlin in full force. A vast pile of irregular shapes and surfaces enclosing 24 rooms, the house was a lavish personal display exploiting the architectural possibilities opened up by wealth and central heating. Complexity of form—tower, turret, gables, and bays—is reinforced by the grand profusion of detail in surface textures, mounting in intensity as the eye rises across the panelled gables and molded cornices to the patterned tiles of roof and tower.

The impact satisfied. Pride of achievement was evident in every line: the Johnsons had made it. Albert H. Johnson enjoyed his house for 14 years. He was killed in a train wreck in Colorado in 1899. Charles Martin Hall bought the place in 1911 and gave it to the college. It was used for the Oberlin Academy till 1916, and for a college dormitory since.

In 1981 preservationist Steven McQuillin, a recent Oberlin graduate, arranged a period repainting of the house which brought back to it some of the passing glory it had enjoyed ten decades before.

LYMAN HALL HOUSE
209 West College

Lyman Bronson Hall, an Oberlin graduate of 1872 who returned to join the faculty five years later, was one of the more vigorous and public-spirited professors over his long tenure at the college. An ardent prohibitionist as a young man, he was also one of three Oberlin professors to bolt the Republican party for Grover Cleveland in 1884, a daring choice in those days. In later years Hall mixed a strong concern for current events and seminar research into his teaching of American history. His diaries, now in the College Archives, are a vivid window on the life of college and town around the century's turn.

His house was a striking addition to West College Street, an urbane brick mansion rising from a high foundation on its narrow corner lot, graced with stylish verandas, eaves, and bargeboard on the north gable. The mason Marvin Teachout, whose mansard home on North Pleasant had brought a similar note of cosmopolitan elegance to the village 18 years before, did the brickwork. Teachout died from injuries suffered when he fell from the scaffolding of Hall's house as it neared completion in the summer of 1885.

131

**GRANDISON
COTTAGE
167 Morgan**

In the fall of 1885 the contractor in charge of building Peters Hall, John Decker of Sandusky, built this little cottage for one of his important craftsmen, a stonecutter named Alexander Grandison. Presumably Grandison worked on Peters, Talcott, and Baldwin (all of which Decker's firm constructed) while living here. About the time they were finished, Grandison left town, and three years later grocer Thomas Bails moved in with his family.

Bertha Bails, the grocer's daughter, graduated from the college in 1908. She lived here the rest of her life, serving as a lab assistant in the college botany department between the two world wars. Neighbors recall her as a shrewd, spirited, and somewhat eccentric woman. She lived frugally, kept big gardens around her house, ate one meal a day at the Oberlin Inn, and treated herself to a new Buick every other year. She died in 1959. The college acquired her house, painted it white, and began renting it to faculty.

The place returned to private care in 1975, and a renovation got underway in sympathy with its vernacular Gothic associations. The snug interior is filled with attractive hardware—carved stone fireplace, fine woodwork, large sliding doors, and intricate brass hinges and knobs. These make it a small domestic museum of nineteenth-century decorative design.

McKEE-SIMS HOUSE
197 Elm

Uriah McKee, instructor in penmanship at the college, had this house built in 1886. It anticipated a number of early twentieth-century style trends, including a horizontal ramble in its massing, jerkinhead dormers, and roof lines of gentle pitch. Its exposed corner location on a cramped site made its inhabitants noticeable folks.

Most prominent among them was Newell Sims, a spry little sociologist who bought this house soon after joining the faculty in 1924 and kept it until his death in 1965. Professor Sims was a pioneering student of Midwestern small-town mores, a prolific scholar, and a lively iconoclast. Tales gathered around him, including the story of his encounter with Esther B. Taylor, Oberlin's sternest prohibitionist in modern times. It seems that one day Sims stepped into his backyard to put an empty wine bottle in his trash can. He spied Mrs. Taylor walking toward him along Cedar Street from her home on Forest. Crouching behind his bayberry hedge, he poked the bottle out through the hedge onto the sidewalk, and waited. The august temperance leader spotted the bottle, picked it up in disgust, and tossed it back over the hedge. Sims solemnly rose and admonished her, "Mrs. Taylor, I don't mind your drinking in public, but please don't throw your bottles in my yard."

**CARPENTER BLOCK
Corner of College
and Main**

The 1880s were a decade for spectacular down-town fires. Another major blaze swept through in May 1886, this one leaving the collection of frame buildings on the southwest corner of the main intersection in ashes. Gone with the rest was old Oberlin Hall, the town's first perma-nent building, which housed the entire facili-ties of the college from 1833 to 1835. It had been used for commercial purposes since 1860. Amid rumors of arson in the wake of the fire, plans were quickly laid for a new brick block on the corner. Architect Frank Weary, then in the thick of a booming business with Oberlin clients, prepared the design. The building, called the Carpenter Block after its principal backers, went up gradually over the next sev-eral years. Its stages can be detected in the three tones of brick used along the College Street facade. A novel feature was the second-story double bay looking out over the street toward the Historic Elm. Plastic store fronts dating from the 1960s confuse the unity of the block which was, all things considered, one of Frank Weary's more restrained performances.

BEDORTHA HOUSE
124 East College

William Bedortha was a hometown boy who made good, in a modest sort of way. The son of an early Oberlin cabinetmaker, he started out as a printer's apprentice with the village newspaper after the Civil War, managed the paper for a while, and then—after reading law under Judge John Steele—was admitted to the bar in 1880. He won quick success as a lawyer and realtor, and swung much weight in local business circles by the turn of the century. In his last years he was attorney to the college.

His house, built in 1886, was a rather tardy exercise in gabled Gothic, a style that had flourished elsewhere back in the 1850s. The treatment of the main gable facing the street, with its vertical siding and small arched window framed by a decorative bargeboard, is a notable feature. Bedortha built the one-story wing to the west a little later to accommodate his mother.

After they passed from the scene, the house served as a rooming house for college athletes. In September 1916 most of the students living here were suspended for forming a secret society—a jarring scandal that ruined the Oberlin football team. (Oberlin lost to Ohio State that fall, 128 to 0.) For 40 years after that banker George W. Morris and family made their home here. Then it became the last site of the Oberlin School of Commerce, which built a brick classroom annex in 1960. When that school folded in 1975, the property reverted to college student housing.

135

WATERWORKS
Morgan

This was the state of the art in waterworks at the turn of the century. The opening of the Parsons Road reservoir in 1961 turned it into a historical relic. The vaguely archaeological aura of its pigeon-spattered stonework inspires many fancy tales about its origin. Some call it Oberlin's answer to Stonehenge.

The complex dates from the 1880s, when concern about polluted wells and cisterns and the threat of typhoid fever persuaded village authorities to plan a safe, modern municipal water system. Adequate reserves for fighting fires were also hoped for. Careful surveys ended in a decision to tap the Vermilion River for a pure supply. A team of Italian immigrant ditch diggers, imported from Pittsburgh, worked through the summer of 1887, laying the connections between river, reservoir, pump house, and village subscribers. Though homeowners were slow to sign up, the system went into operation by Christmas, and its capacity expanded steadily thereafter. The 40-foot stone tower, topped by a tall steel storage tank, was completed in 1893, and a second reservoir was added in 1916. In 1903 waterworks trustees installed a municipal lime-soda water softening plant, touted as the first in the United States. Pleasant landscaping and forestation of the surrounding acres, and the technical advances built into the facilities, brought wide renown to the waterworks in the early decades of this century.

Obsolescence has improved the enigmatic charm of the stone tower. It continues to excite curiosity among newcomers and tourists, who wonder what mysterious purposes it might serve. Only the pigeons know for sure.

GASWORKS ROUND HOUSE
South Main Street

This battered relic of the gaslight era is Oberlin's best example of industrial functionalism in nineteenth-century architecture. It is also a reminder of the quick pace of technological change in urban America.

It was built with some 300,000 bricks in 1889 by the Oberlin Gas Lighting Company (Albert H. Johnson, president) as a storage holder for locally manufactured coal gas. It made possible a huge expansion of capacity for an enterprise which Samuel Plumb had launched back in 1858. Oberlin was the first town in the area to enjoy gaslit streets. But in the 1880s gas began yielding to electricity as the main source of public illumination. Oberlin moved toward conversion with some caution. "Many of the cities are having such sad experiences with electricity," the local paper noted, "that the smaller towns which have been debating the matter of adopting that system of lighting will doubtless be content with the old and less dangerous methods."

Was electricity here to stay? What were the costs? Should the town wait until it could build its own public power plant? The village council wrestled earnestly with these issues for years. Meanwhile Albert H. Johnson, who had not become a millionaire by fighting Progress, proceeded with his own quiet conversion. His Oberlin Gas Lighting Company turned into the Oberlin Gas & Electric Company, the wires were strung, and the contract signed. On the night of September 28, 1893, Oberlin's streets glowed with Johnson's electric lights.

Although coal gas continued to be manufactured for heating, the exploitation of natural gas deposits in northern Ohio around the turn of the century soon made the older fuel obsolete, and the gasworks buildings began their slow decay.

The west side of Woodland, land once owned
by President Charles G. Finney, is thick with
college rental properties—ordinary nineteenth-
century wood frame houses, painted white and
rented out to students and young faculty. This
homely sample suggests the rich fund of forgotten social history that lies behind their
doors. Built in the 1880s, it was in 1914 the
home of Mary Breckenridge, mother of conservatory professor William Breckenridge. She
took in roomers, and one of them that fall was
a freshman named Edward Willkie. When Edward got into academic trouble, his older
brother, Wendell, a recent graduate of Indiana
University, came to live with him and help him
out. Wendell audited chemistry classes as a
special student in his spare time. Both brothers
left after one semester.

Twenty-six years later, when Wendell Willkie
ran against Franklin Roosevelt for the presidency, he took Oberlin by storm. The big,
rumpled Hoosier, whistle-stopping in Elyria in
October 1940, said of his Oberlin days, "I
didn't know anything about chemistry when I
came to Oberlin, and I didn't know much about
it when I left." On election day he lost to FDR
but swept Oberlin, taking 68 percent of the
town vote and 64 percent of the college student

139

straw poll, a sizable jump over Alf Landon's showing in 1936.

In 1943, on his crusade to swing the Republican party from isolationism toward the risks of living in "One World," Willkie came back to Oberlin to receive an honorary degree. In an impromptu talk after the ceremony, he dwelt on themes that gripped his mind in the last year of his life. "How the world goes," he said, "depends absolutely on how America goes, and in the final analysis on how the Middle West will go—and here in the Middle West the quiet little villages will decide."

Then he embroidered on his youthful Oberlin experience. "I had a perfectly delightful time here," he said, noting that his special status had freed him from many college social rules. "The fact that I could smoke seemed to make me very popular with the girls." But the smell of his tobacco clung to his brother's clothing, and Edward fell suspect and was expelled. College records are mute on the tale.

FINLEY-DICK HOUSE
195 South Professor

Rising from its little hilltop overlooking Plum Creek, this comfortable, multigabled home has housed a variety of notable villagers over the past century. Scratched in an old glass windowpane on the south wing of the house is the name "Finley." This was Captain Peter Finley, a hearty Canadian Scot who settled in Oberlin soon after the Civil War. An 1870 map shows him living here. Finley and his sons were mariners; he mastered a Great Lakes iron ore boat on runs between Lake Superior and Cleveland in the 1870s. In 1883 he retired from the lakes and ran a village meat market until his death in 1906.

Matthew Dick, a merchant prominent in local politics, bought the hilltop property from Finley in 1886. The present appearance of the house dates from Dick's extensive remodelling in 1889.

Twenty years later Professor William J. Hutchins took ownership. Hutchins taught homiletics in the graduate school of technology from 1907 to 1920. These were the years when Oberlin bent the twig in Hutchins's son, Robert Maynard Hutchins, who went on to fame and controversy as a moving presence in American higher education. Growing up by the banks of Plum Creek, young Hutchins entered the college in 1915. He later remembered it as having "the worst climate, the hardest seats, and the silliest rules of any institution in the world." He also recalled receiving "the best teaching I have seen or experienced anywhere." When the

141

United States entered World War I, Hutchins left Oberlin to join the army ambulance corps. He later finished college at Yale. Meanwhile his father left Oberlin to become president of Berea College. The son followed the father into college administration, first at Yale and then as president of the University of Chicago, where he tried long and hard to plant his version of educational utopia.

Between the two world wars, 195 South Professor was the home of Victor and Josephine Lytle, teachers at the conservatory. Tree surgeon Art Salo and his wife Mildred bought the house in 1943. To take advantage of what may be the best view in town, in 1956 the Salos installed the picture window to the left of the front porch. As a schoolgirl back in the 1920s, Mrs. Salo helped deliver milk from her family farm, Clark Jersey Dairy, just west of Oberlin. Her route included two quarts daily to her future home.

In 1889 several young members of the conservatory faculty bought lots toward the west end of Elm, in an area known as Hawley's orchard. Soon a cluster of new homes was going up, each house a variation on the popular Shingle Style of the day. None was more eye-catching than that built for Edgar G. Sweet, professor of pianoforte and singing. The house was constructed by contractor Charles Glenn, who was the busiest home builder in Oberlin toward the end of the century. Professor Sweet had a hand in the design, which melds a complex array of curved and angled shapes. The master bedroom under its squat tower, leading out to a second-story porch, was the decisive feature in a nicely managed composition. (The unusual round-cornered frames of this porch have been slightly altered since.) Some of the ideas built into the house look as if they might have borrowed from Henry Hobson Richardson's influential 1883 Stoughton house in Cambridge, Massachusetts. In any event, it is perhaps the most innovative of Oberlin's homegrown contributions to the eclectic Queen Anne phase in American architecture.

For years the young conservatory crowd enlivened neighborhood social life with its Haphazard Club, named for the unscheduled geniality of its meetings. After World War I, with their two daughters grown and married, the Sweets built a new home still farther west on Elm, and sold the house at 279 to chemistry professor

143

Alfred Lothrop. His son Richard grew up here, and in 1960 returned to live in his boyhood home.

Charles W. Morrison was another young conservatory professor who bought a lot on the
west end of Elm in 1889. Like each of its
brown-shingled neighbors, his house stood
apart with a special mood of its own. The low
slope of its roof lines, its broad eaves and half-
timbered gables, and the angular woodwork of
its rambling porch make it a choice example of
stick-and-shingle styling, which enjoyed a national vogue in the 1880s. The local newspaper
reported breathlessly that the interior was
decorated in high fashion "by a lady artist
from Cincinnati."

Professor Morrison replaced Fenelon Rice as
director of the conservatory and held that post
from 1902 to 1924. A splendid piano teacher
and a man of merry charm, he was remembered by neighbors for the loud gaiety of his
household. The next conservatory director,
Frank Shaw, succeeded Morrison in residence
at 290 Elm as well.

The contractor for this house back in 1889,
Charles Glenn, was the eldest son of a
Virginia-born Negro barber. His mother was a
German immigrant. Glenn did a flourishing
business in local home building before he died
of tuberculosis in 1903. His younger brother
Herbert later became superintendent of car-
pentry for the college. Herbert Glenn's daughter, schoolteacher Elizabeth Glenn Thomas,

cracked the color barrier in Oberlin's public school system in 1942, and taught until retirement in 1975.

SHURTLEFF COTTAGE
159 South Professor

This was General Shurtleff's third and final contribution to the movement of village architecture across the Gilded Age. Having sold his first home (the Shurtleff-Monroe house, now standing by the conservatory parking lot) to James Monroe in 1870, he next built an elegant Italianate house on Elm Street (later known as Elmwood, and pulled down in 1963 to make way for South Hall). In 1892 he hired the firm of Weary & Kramer to design this fashionable Shingle Style home on the former site of Oberlin's first graveyard. The long arc of the north gable roof, sweeping down past cozy balconied windows and over the porch, is the most striking feature of an elaborate design, and is best viewed from the pathway along Plum Creek.

Giles Shurtleff, who was born in Quebec just north of the Vermont line, graduated from Oberlin College in 1859. He was a strong-willed antislavery man, and he fought a lively Civil War. Captured while leading the Monroe Rifles (an Oberlin company named for James Monroe) in western Virginia in August 1861, he spent a year in Confederate prisons. After release in a prisoner exchange he shunned medical discharge and took command of a black regiment organized by fellow Oberlinian John Mercer Langston. Shurtleff led the regiment through several fierce battles in northern Virginia, was badly wounded, and came out a brigadier general. Life was calmer after that. He devoted it to teaching Latin and raising money for his alma mater. He held several important admin-

147

istrative posts at the college before his retirement. In 1898, 33 years after Appomattox, he got out his sword and faded blue uniform and posed for sculptor Emily Ewing Peck, who in good Oberlin fashion relieved the general of his sword. The resulting neo-classical statue has stood on the lawn in front of Shurtleff, amusing college students since its unveiling in 1911.

The college converted his home into a dormitory in 1912.

ROWLAND HOUSE
152 East College

Built in 1892 for druggist Thad Rowland, this brick-and-shingle Queen Anne home presented the village with a ripe display of domestic finery. Viewed from the street, the radial stickwork in the porch pediment, the subtle waffle pattern of circles and squares gracing the second-story bay window, and the climactic Eastlake geometry in the main gable form a lavish ornamental mix. The three-dimensional texture of these details is dramatized by the deep curve of the corbels flanking the bay.

The interior entry room sustains the Eastlake motif in glossy panels of rubbed oak. The ceiling and staircase in the room are a showpiece of high Victorian craftsmanship. It is one of four first-floor living spaces surrounding a massive central chimney shaft, each room warmed by a distinctive fireplace.

Thad Rowland reached affluence by filling the quiet private needs of sober Oberlin. Soon after his arrival in town in the early 1870s, he was running a popular drugstore on South Main Street. Late nineteenth-century druggists often had a corner on illicit liquor traffic in dry towns, and Rowland's under-the-counter remedies brought him a thriving business despite periodic crackdowns by local prohibitionists.

Warm-blooded and gregarious, Rowland enjoyed life in ways that many villagers must have frowned on. He profited nicely from shrewd real estate ventures, played the horses, and loved a good dog race. He also belonged to the wrong political party. "He was born a Democrat," the town paper noted, "and has never recovered from this minor ailment." His reputation survived his sins, however, and improved with age. Acquaintances remembered Rowland as a silver-haired old gentleman, elegant in his white linen suit, white Panama hat, and gold-crowned cane, strolling the downtown streets, hailing friends and happily checking out his commercial properties.

Walter and Doris Gorske kept the house and grounds in mint condition after taking possession in 1956.

ANDREWS HOUSE
195 Forest

As a big burst of Queen Anne exuberance, this house is surpassed only by Johnson House on South Professor. The intricate play of chimney stack and gabled bay rising on the western wall is just one example of architectural fancy in its composition. The house has commanded its corner lot since the summer of 1893, when it went up for conservatory professor George W. Andrews.

Andrews and the conservatory came of age together. The connection lasted over 60 years, from 1869 when he began studying at age 8 under Fenelon B. Rice until his retirement in 1931 at age 70. As a boy he played piano, violin, and trombone in the conservatory orchestra, at a time when the double bass player was an East Oberlin farmer and a local tailor played clarinet. Andrews joined the faculty in 1882 to teach organ. Thereafter he directed the orchestra for 20 years and the Musical Union for over three decades. As teacher, composer, conductor, and performer, he had the knack of doing things well, and early on he won a national reputation. His son later told friends that the family home was financed from the fee Andrews earned for playing the organ at the Chicago World's Fair of 1893. Locally he was long remembered for his inspired amen improvisations on the organ in Finney Chapel.

His daughter Esther (Mrs. Reber Johnson) maintained the home until 1964, when it was sold to the college and divided into apartments.

151

In 1977 conservatory oboist James Caldwell and his wife Catharina bought the house and restored its former glow.

MEAD HOUSE
137 Elm

The early history of this big house is linked with many people—most of them Meads—who once were very prominent in academic life at Oberlin and elsewhere. The place was built in 1872 for Hiram Mead, who taught sacred rhetoric at the college. His wife, Elizabeth Storrs Mead, had an important career of her own ahead, but at the time she was raising their children, Alice and George. Alice graduated from Oberlin in 1879, George in 1883.

When Hiram Mead died in 1881 his widow vacated their home, and James K. Newton, Oberlin's first full-time professor of modern languages, moved in. He needed a large house to board students who could live together and converse in French and German. Thus Oberlin's first language dorm was born.

Meanwhile the Meads kept busy. Elizabeth, after teaching English for a while at the college, returned to her native New England. In 1890 she became the first president of Mount Holyoke College, and spent the next decade transforming that place from a tiny female seminary into a top-flight modern women's college. Her son, George Herbert Mead, who as an Oberlin undergraduate rebelled against President Fairchild's dogmatic teachings in moral philosophy, went on to graduate study at Harvard and Leipzig. In 1894 he joined the faculty at the new University of Chicago. His scholarship over the next 40 years in social psychology and philosophy left a lasting mark on sociological theory. Daughter Alice stayed in Oberlin and

153

married Albert Temple Swing, a German-trained professor of church history. They made their home at 90 South Professor (since destroyed). In 1924 they endowed the Mead-Swing Foundation, which ever since has brought distinguished lecturers in science and religion to the campus.

The memoirs of their son Raymond about his boyhood testify to Oberlin's irksome moral grip. "As I now look back on it, a great part of my life at Oberlin was devoted to a conflict within myself between good and bad," he wrote. "I wanted to be good, but it was too much for me." He made it through one year at the college, breaking as many rules as possible. He smoked, played cards, joined a secret society, cut class, and was finally suspended in 1905 for flunking French. He went on to a crowded career in journalism and ultimately became a household name as foreign correspondent and radio commentator Raymond Gram Swing. Mollified by his success, Oberlin gave him an honorary degree in 1940, and made him a trustee in 1946.

The Mead's old home on Elm Street meanwhile continued to be used as a boardinghouse for college students. Its present appearance dates from 1893, when a fire destroyed the roof and the house was remodelled, receiving a symmetricality it lacked before, and enlarged to the rear. Between the two world wars it was known as Gulde House, a dormitory for 30 women. In the 1970s it was converted to college-owned rental apartments whose residents, many of them divorced, renamed it Alimony Arms.

SEVERANCE HOUSE
68 South Professor

Local housing history took a fresh turn when James R. Severance commissioned this striking gambrel-roofed house in 1894. Severance, a Vermont-born Oberlin graduate, taught elocution at the college in the 1870s. A versatile fellow, he turned his hand to mechanical invention and developed improvements on the harvesting machine which were picked up by the Chicago-based McCormick empire and exhibited at the Chicago World's Fair. After a decade in the farm machinery business, Severance returned to replace Giles Shurtleff as college treasurer in 1894.

He removed the old house on this lot and hired a Chicago architect (name unrecorded, possibly Joseph Lyman Silsbee) to design his new home. The result was a bold composition in sandstone and shingle that reached back to the Dutch colonial country house for inspiration. Its ground-hugging lines are dramatized by the deep swing of the roof kicking out over a broad porch terrace. Generous dimensions in rooms and windows and unusually fine woodwork distinguish the interior. The house took 14 months to complete to the owner's satisfaction.

Treasurer Severance managed college business operations with skill until his death in 1916. His daughter Julia, an artist of some promise, pursued her work in a glass-roofed studio off the stone barn to the rear. In 1911 she designed a new college seal. The largest version of this seal graces the lobby of Wilder Hall.

In 1940 she sold the family house to Ben and Gertrude Lewis, who lived here until 1984. Ben Lewis, a nationally eminent economist, taught at the college from 1925 to 1967, a stretch interrupted by many stints of government service. A scholars' bridge in Mudd Learning Center is named for him.

DOOLITTLE HOUSE
291 Elm

This was the third variant on the Shingle Style to be completed near the corner of Elm and Prospect in the 1890s. With its symmetry of line and fenestration, well-defined cornice, and broad hip roof, it reflects the revival of eighteenth-century colonial influences which tinged American architectural taste near the century's turn. It was built for Charles P. Doolittle in the summer of 1897.

C. P. Doolittle taught violoncello and harmony at the conservatory from 1885 to 1911. With a versatility that seems laughable from the perspective of our specialists' age, he doubled as college superintendent of buildings and grounds for 18 years.

Doolittle was a great promoter in the bicycle craze that swept Oberlin and the nation in the 1890s. He spent the entire summer of 1895 laying out bicycle paths around Tappan Square and northward out of town toward Lake Erie. His enthusiasm earned him the happy nickname "Cinder Path" Doolittle.

Historian Robert S. Fletcher bought the Doolittle house in 1931 and lived here with his wife Mary Elizabeth until his death in 1959. Fletcher's history of early Oberlin, to which he devoted 20 years of work, set standards of scholarship and storytelling in local social history that may never be surpassed.

157

TANK
110 East College

In the decades around the turn of the century, Oberlin served as a kind of staging area for missionary Christianity overseas. The college contributed many recruits for the cause, and the town became a haven for its noncombatants. Aging ministers, missionaries, and their widowed spouses retired in large numbers to the village, and the small children of those in the field were often kept here. In 1897 the Tank Home for Missionary Children was completed to lodge these youngsters.

A vast, rambling structure of brick and shingle wrapped by a deep veranda, its interior was a mosaic of varied spaces finished in sycamore, oak, maple, and pine. The design came from Cleveland architect F. A. Coburn, and the busy Oberlin team of Glenn and Copeland were the builders.

The dormitory was a gift from the estate of Caroline Tank. She was the widow of Nils Otto Tank, a wealthy son of Norwegian gentry, who had worked as a missionary in Dutch Guiana in the 1840s and later founded a Moravian religious commune of Norwegian emigrants in northern Wisconsin (near Green Bay) before his death in 1864.

In 1922, with missionary children thinning out, the college acquired Tank for use as a women's dormitory. It became one of the college's popular co-op dorms in 1963.

REAMER-DUDLEY BARN
Route 10 West

Barns are winning more attention from architectural historians than they used to. Among the choice local examples is this pleasant dairy barn, built for Daniel P. Reamer in 1897. Reamer was a Pennsylvania-born merchant who ran general stores in Wellington and Oberlin before moving to Leavenworth, Kansas in 1872. Then he prospered as a travelling salesman for a Chicago wholesale furniture house, supplying banks and public buildings throughout the Middle West.

Reamer returned to make his home in Oberlin on South Professor in the late 1870s. Twenty years later when nearing retirement, he decided to invest his savings in 60 head of prize Jersey cattle. The queen of the herd was Croton Countess, who made up to 30 pounds of butter per week.

Reamer's new barn to house the herd won notice both for its modern facilities and its fancy Swiss Gothic styling. The plans probably came from Reamer's nephew, Daniel A. Reamer, a trained architect. Notable details include the three tiers of wood siding along its outside walls, dominated by a broad middle band of roundheaded panels; a rich yard-wide bargeboard hung along the northern gable; and the trio of capped ventilator cones along the roof ridge.

Reamer apparently intended to build a house nearby, but death in 1900 intervened. Seven years later the Dudley family, which had long farmed across the road, bought the property, and Ben Dudley carried on the dairy operation with his sons through the 1950s. Today the barn is used for storage. It remains one of the fine rural buildings in the township, and went on the National Register in 1979.

FIRST HOSPITAL
21 South Cedar

This boxy, hip-roofed house with attic dormers and broad front porch, a design very popular at the turn of the century, has a history more complex than most. It went up in the summer of 1898 as a home and student rooming house for Mary Spear. She was the widow of Charles Vinal Spear, donor of the college library that once stood on Tappan Square bearing his name. In 1903 Mrs. Spear sold to another widow, Alice Williams, whose husband was one of the Oberlin missionaries killed in the Boxer Rebellion. Among Mrs. Williams's student roomers was H. H. Kung, who graduated from the college in 1906, and later achieved vast wealth as a banker in his native China.

In 1907, the Oberlin Hospital Association leased the house from Mrs. Williams and converted it for use as the town's first hospital, a stopgap measure to meet a desperate local need. The fast pace of medical modernization made the facility inadequate from the outset. After World War I, when babies began to be born in hospitals on a regular basis, and home quarantine for contagious diseases became obsolete, the need for a real hospital was clear.

When Allen Memorial Hospital finally opened in 1925, the Cedar Street house reverted to domestic use. Mrs. Williams returned to live here, and in 1946 her faithful old student roomer, H. H. Kung, bought the house and deeded it to the Oberlin Shansi Memorial Association on the understanding that Mrs. Williams could stay in residence for the rest of her life. She died in 1952 at age 91.

The house became the home of religion professor Clyde Holbrook in 1956. The Holbrooks expanded their living room to the south, in part to accommodate their sociable Great Dane, Jonah. When they sold to the college in 1966 and moved out to a new home on Hawthorne Drive, 21 South Cedar began to deteriorate under use by short-term renters. That decline was reversed in 1979, when history professor Ronald DiCenzo bought the house and started applying his "sweat equity" to the property indoors and out, to the delight of neighbors. Pride in ownership does wonders for a house.

HALL SISTERS
HOUSE
280 Elm

The history of this house includes two separate chapters about personal philanthropy in Oberlin.

After Charles Martin Hall scored his major experimental breakthrough in working out the modern process for making aluminum in 1886, his sister Julia gave him crucial help in his tough struggle to win patents and backers for his process. After that his fortune was secure. He left Oberlin to live in Niagara Falls, New York, but his hometown roots and family ties remained intact. Aluminum money built this house for Julia and two other sisters, Edith and Louie, in 1901—the first of many Hall-financed gifts in Oberlin. Ample and substantial in appearance, but shunning gaudy display, it somehow reflects the essential modesty of the Halls' Oberlin origins. In fact it represents an architectural updating of the simple wood frame gabled homes that lined the early village streets by the dozens.

By the time of Hall's death in 1914, his sisters had all left Oberlin. In 1928 Gladys Sellew bought the house for her elderly mother to live in. Born and educated in Cincinnati, Gladys Sellew spent most of her career teaching nursing and sociology in Washington, D.C. Her field research on the black family made her an expert on housing problems among poor minorities. When she settled in Oberlin in 1958 to pursue a vigorous retirement, she put her training and personal savings to work subsidizing home ownership among low-income families. She built some 15 homes, most of them located in the southeast quadrant on Gladys Court (named for her), and sold them at low interest rates. She improved many other homes at cost. Meanwhile she opened her house at 280 Elm rent-free to student roomers, asking only that they earn their keep with chores around the house and yard—a latter-day version of the manual labor arrangements in early Oberlin. In 1971 she was given the college's first Distinguished Community Service Award. She died in 1977.

OLD BARROWS
207 South Professor

Old Barrows recalls in several ways the influence of Chicago cosmopolitanism on Oberlin at the century's turn. It was built for Oberlin president John Henry Barrows in 1901. Barrows had come to Oberlin three years before, after a vigorous career promoting efforts to turn Christianity into a global religious force—"the army of the Lord," as he called it, "which stands with faces fronting the dawn, holding in their hands the 'white shields of expectation.' " He had taught comparative religions at the new University of Chicago and organized a World's Parliament of Religions for the Chicago World's Fair. An urbane, captivating figure and an able fund raiser, he succeeded during his brief tenure in pulling Oberlin out of deep financial trouble. He brought a fresh breeze to a community which he privately regarded as somewhat static and provincial. Soon after his arrival he wrote sardonically to a friend about "the wild delights and Bacchanalian Orgies of the Oberlin Sphinx."

The White City of the Chicago World's Fair helped inspire a wave of neo-classicism in American building. In public architecture and city planning this reached back to the models of imperial Rome. In domestic housing it revived a taste for eighteenth-century Georgian styling. Chicago architect Howard Van Doren Shaw caught the latter trend in his design for Barrows's home. The imposing central portico with its white Ionic pillars against red brick was a conscious effort to summon the stately

165

traditions of the colonial Virginia plantation.

Barrows caught pneumonia while on a tour of eastern cities and died just seven months after the house was finished. The college bought it for dormitory use in 1916. Its demolition was averted in 1963 when Professor Warren Taylor led a community campaign to prevent the Firelands Retirement Center from rising on the site. This campaign was the first local assertion for preservation purposes of the Supreme Court's 1954 finding that citizens could act to insure that "the community should be beautiful as well as healthy, spacious as well as clean, well-balanced as well as carefully patrolled."

HOWARD APARTMENTS
18 North Pleasant

Oberlin never grew at quite the pace its boomers hoped for. Still, a variety of pressures converged around 1900 to create a need for more housing space near the village center. The arrival of speedy interurban electric trolley service, with the main stop at the intersection of College and Main, tended to tighten living patterns and raise the value on remaining downtown lots. A high turnover in the local population combined with rising building costs to place a premium on scarce rental property.

To meet these urban needs, the Oberlin Realty Company in 1904 built the town's first modern apartment building—the Howard. An eight-unit complex, it faced both North Pleasant and a new street (Willard Court) cut in just to the west. The apartments were spacious, well appointed, and equipped with the very latest kitchen conveniences, including enamelled sinks, gas ranges, and built-in refrigerators which could be supplied with milk and ice by outside delivery. To meet ventilation and privacy problems—long the bane of city tenements—arcades and breezeways interlaced the units. It was a pleasing and successful design solution. The exterior appearance, with its two-story galleries, oddly recalls a West Indian arrangement first imported to this country along the Carolina coast in the early eighteenth century.

The Howard has been doing a brisk business for over eight decades. Now owned by the college, and a little worn at the seams, the Howard mainly serves young faculty newcomers, some of whom no doubt dream of living in a modern apartment complex.

GIBSON'S BAKERY
23 West College

Gibson's Bakery is the oldest family business in town. Gibson pastries have been fortifying the diet of Oberlinians, especially high school and college students, since the presidency of Grover Cleveland. Mr. and Mrs. O. C. Gibson opened a pie shop on West College Street in 1888, and their sons Bert and Cass sold popcorn, peanuts, and taffy at a stand on the main intersection during the peak years of Oberlin's interurban trolley boom. The present Gibson store opened in 1905. The town's first movie theater operated on the floor above from 1907 to 1910. By the 1920s, several thousand loaves of bread were being baked daily at Gibson's and delivered around town by truck from door to door.

Cass Gibson retired in 1946. Four years later Bert Gibson and his sons Harold and Allyn remodelled the family store to its present appearance. The street facade, with its sleek black glass and streamlined aluminum panels and lettering, brought a classy touch of the Moderne to Oberlin's downtown.

Bert Gibson made up his last batch of Christmas candy in December 1975 and died six months later at age 98. Allyn Gibson carries on today, and the students keep coming.

LAUDERLEIGH HALL
135 West College

The appearance in 1907 of this handsome stucco house, with its red tile roof and bold double brackets, brought a note of twentieth-century sophistication to its block. Elements of neo-Georgian symmetry and Mediterranean warmth graced the structure inside and out. It was built for a village dentist, Harry Lauderdale, and his wife Mabel, an aspiring artist, who ran it as a student boardinghouse through the 1920s.

In 1930 Lauderleigh Hall became La Maison Francaise, and served as a college language dorm for the next 23 years. Some 20 women lived here and dined in French with 20 men. Together they carried on a lively social life under the eye of a resident directrice and members of the French faculty. The festive rituals of the house included an annual baptism of each student room by the department chairman, decked out in academic regalia for the occasion.

The collegiate gaiety ended in 1953 when Mr. and Mrs. Glen Ritter bought the house and turned it into seven private apartments. Since 1972 the college has owned the property and kept it in excellent trim.

MOSHER HOUSE
281 Forest

Among Oberlin's earliest and most impressive neo-Tudor homes was this house, built for Professor William E. Mosher in the summer of 1907. The neo-Tudor style, obliquely derived from the half-timbered cottages of Elizabethan England, stressed broad-angled outlines, attention to surface textures, and strong accents of light and dark in the framing of windows and doors. The Mosher house rises gracefully in three tiers from a first story of stuccoed concrete to a second story of dark shingles to a flaring hip roof pierced by shed dormers of generous proportion. Its composition affirmed the conservative confidence of mainstream domestic architecture in the years before World War I.

That war broke Mosher's professional life in two. He had graduated from Oberlin in 1899, taken a Ph.D. at the University of Halle in Germany, and started teaching German at his alma mater in 1904. Three years later, at age 30, he became head of his department, built his new house, and bought an automobile.

His career prospered till the moment America entered the war against Germany in 1917. Hatred of the Hun soon devastated all things German in the popular mind, and Oberlin was not exempt from this passion. Enrollments in college German classes evaporated, the department fell apart, and Mosher left Oberlin for the New School for Social Research in New York City. There he transformed himself from

171

a German scholar into an expert on public administration. In 1924 he went to Syracuse University to organize the Maxwell School of Citizenship and Public Affairs, the first school of its kind in the country. In the 1930s he won national prominence as an authority on the regulation and ownership of electric utilities. His intellectual bounce awed old Oberlin friends. Professor Louis Lord, presenting him for an honorary degree in 1940, said of Mosher, "He believes everything more strenuously than I believe anything."

Mosher's Forest Street house has been the home of several notable people over the years, including newspaper editor and village historian W. H. Phillips, sociologist L. Guy Brown, Dr. W. H. Turner, and sports radical Jack Scott. Kim and Larry Buell bought the house in 1973.

A substantial housing boom hit Oberlin in 1908. Early that spring, plans were announced for a new residential development on the western edge of town near the site of an abandoned racetrack. C. D. Reamer, a former Oberlin merchant who had moved to Chattanooga, Tennessee, returned to organize the venture with help from his son, architect Daniel A. Reamer. They envisioned a sequence of elegant homes on spacious lawns along a macadam street with a massive stone gateway at one end and a small circular park at the other. A back-door delivery drive wrapped in a U-shape around the whole. It was an attractive scheme. The lots sold quickly and the first houses went up that summer. People came in their buggies from miles around to look over Oberlin's rich new residential Midway.

The home of Charles W. Savage was the earliest completed. Designed by Cleveland architect Charles Hopkinson, it is a late version of the stick-and-shingle Queen Anne style, rather more symmetrically organized than earlier compositions in this vein. Savage and his family moved in before the house was finished, and his daughters recalled climbing to their rooms by ladder while carpenters hammered away below.

Savage was one of the college's more memorable sons. As a student in the early 1890s he was lionized for his gridiron skills. One autumn afternoon in 1892 he ran the length of

173

the field in Ann Arbor to clinch Oberlin's first, last, and only victory over the University of Michigan. After graduate work at Harvard and Columbia, he became Oberlin's first director of athletics. He was a national leader in the drive launched by President Theodore Roosevelt to clean up the game of football. During his three decades on the Oberlin faculty he waged a steady campaign to make amateur, competitive athletics an integral part of a college education.

When Savage died in 1957, a sports writer for the *Cleveland Plain Dealer* reached fondly back into the past to imagine him approaching the pearly gates—"once again galloping over that Michigan gridiron with the ball tucked under his arm, his straight-arm working to perfection, and the goal posts getting near and nearer and nearer!"

FISKE HOUSE
336 Reamer

From the year of its opening, Reamer Place
served as a display zone for twentieth-century
tastes in domestic architecture. Perhaps the
most innovative house on the block was this
one, completed by realtor and builder William
W. Thompson in the fall of 1908 and sold to
Professor G. Walter Fiske the following spring.
It is Oberlin's earliest and most elaborate version of the new Bungalow Style, a form which
apparently originated in British India and
caught on in southern California just after the
century's turn. Its chief traits were gently
sloped roofs with broad bracketed eaves, deep
verandas, and generous fenestration. Adapted
for a mellow climate, the early American bungalow opened its interior to spacious, airy
rooms. Its inviting lines diminished the distinction between indoors and out, creating a
mood of shadowed accessibility.

In California the brothers Charles and Henry
Greene popularized the new style. Their rustic,
rambling designs were winning notice in architectural journals just as Reamer Place opened
up. This may have served as inspiration for
Daniel A. Reamer, son of the developer of Reamer Place, who was credited at his death in 1927
with having provided plans for all but two of
the street's early houses. A versatile architect,
Reamer was born in Oberlin, attended the Oberlin
academy as a boy, and later fought in the Span-
ish-American War. Little has been learned about
his professional training, but he seems to have

picked up his skills during the five years he spent in Chicago, the center of American architectural creativity, in the 1890s.

Professor Fiske, an Amherst classmate of Calvin Coolidge, taught in the graduate school of theology from 1907 to 1937 and was a prolific author. In 1923 he sold the house to Dr. Whitelaw Morrison, longtime professor of physical education. Morrison in turn sold in 1954 to psychology professor Robert Dixon who with his wife Libby lived here till 1983.

Bungalows tended to contract in size as they multiplied in number across the northern United States in the decade after 1910. One trim, boxy example nearby is 285 Oak, built for college administrator W. F. Bohn in 1913.

ANDRUS HOUSE
251 Forest

The Reverend Jonathan C. Andrus, a former Congregational minister, arrived in town from Massachusetts in 1907 to educate his twin sons at the Oberlin academy and later the college. He promptly commissioned architect Daniel A. Reamer (then much involved in his father's Reamer Place development) to design his Oberlin home. The resulting brick-and-stucco composition, completed in 1908, bears some resemblance to the 1893 William Winslow house in suburban Chicago, one of Frank Lloyd Wright's early domestic creations. Reamer's architectural pedigree remains unknown, but the years he spent in Chicago in the mid-1890s suggest that his training took place there, and the possibility that he was touched by Wright's example, among others, makes for intriguing speculation.

Like the street facade of the Winslow house, the Andrus plan is symmetrical in form and draws attention to the central entry space by setting it apart in clean, decisive outline: doorway flanked by windows, visually defined in a broad rectangular frame. And in both houses the wide overhang of the hip roof seems to hover above its supporting walls. These comparisons need not be pressed too far. The Winslow house was an early stride for Wright in a journey toward fame. Oberlin's Andrus house was one of Reamer's many offerings in the contemporary newness before he lapsed into obscurity.

177

The Andrus twins grew up here, graduated from the college in 1916, and after a year of graduate study headed together for Johns Hopkins, where they earned their M.D.'s in 1921. Edwin Andrus became a heart specialist in Baltimore; William, a surgeon in New York. Together they received honorary degrees from Oberlin in 1941. Their parents remained in town through the early 1920s, directing Browning House, the college infirmary. Then they left to live with their daughter Ruth, a Vassar graduate and Columbia Ph.D. who had a long career in the New York State Department of Education.

From 1966 to 1978 the Andrus house on Forest was the home of Evan and Cindy Nord. Their work in historic preservation, among other causes, is a well-known and appreciated village fact.

FULLERTON HOUSE
318 Reamer

When the sidewalks and first houses on Reamer Place took shape in 1908, the street drew many tempted gazers. One of them was Kemper Fullerton, who had come to the Oberlin faculty from Lane Seminary four years before. Fullerton spent many a summer evening strolling the street with his wife Kate and pondering their budget. Finally he contracted with Cleveland architect Charles W. Hopkinson for a house on Reamer. "The deed is done," he told his diary. "I've wasted an entire month on it and nearly worried myself sick. Hardly the way to begin building a house. But I do hope God will bless it." Completed in 1909, the house added yet another theme to Reamer's growing medley: a handsome English Cottage, serene in stucco and shingle. The Fullertons lived here for the rest of their lives.

No one in Oberlin watched college and country struggle through the next three decades more perceptively than Kemper Fullerton. A deeply learned biblical scholar, liberal in his religious and political views, and a profound cultural conservative, he felt the tight moral assumptions of his youth ripped apart by world war and postwar disillusion. The cultural newness of the 1920s—jazz, Hemingway novels, Watsonian psychology—bothered him. When nearing retirement in 1930, he was asked by the senior class to deliver their commencement address. He wondered what on earth to say. "It is a bewildering world," he mused. "The breakdown

179

of standards along all lines has precipitated a crisis such as the world has not known since the Protestant Reformation. To tell students what to believe at such a time is a difficult thing to do, and they would probably not follow my advice if I did tell them." The address he gave is included in his published essays, a vintage gathering of worried post-Victorian wisdom.

**CARRUTHERS HOUSE
319 Reamer**

In 1948 this substantial neo-Georgian house, built of yellow brick with red tile roof, became the home of the distinguished sociologist George E. Simpson and his wife Eleanor. It is the single architectural reminder of one of Oberlin's remarkable nineteenth-century families. It went up in 1909 for Claudia Straus Carruthers and her husband Will. Mrs. Carruthers was the daughter of August Straus, who was in turn the cousin of Marx Straus, and therein lies a tale.

Back in 1852 Marx Straus, a 23-year-old Jewish immigrant from Germany, came to Oberlin to open a small dry-goods store. Cousin August joined him eight years later. His first job was to gather furs from local farmers. More or less penniless on their arrival, the cousins Straus were soon thriving. Business connections with relatives in New York City enabled them to offer high quality goods in the latest fashions at prices lower than any Oberlin competitor. By the end of the Civil War, Marx Straus was the richest man in town, and possibly the first to smoke cigars in public. He lived in a fancy house, palatial by Oberlin standards, on South Main. It was guarded by a brightly painted cast-iron stag and mastiff standing in the front yard. House and animals have long since disappeared. In 1878 Marx Straus purchased Park House, the original brick Oberlin Inn. He later donated the inn building to the college, a gift valued at $50,000. The present inn replaced the original in 1955.

181

The August Straus family lived on Forest, on land now occupied by dormitories. After cousin Marx moved to Elyria in 1880, August succeeded him as Oberlin's leading clothier. When his daughter Claudia decided to marry village jeweller Will Carruthers, she made Will a happy man. Genial and easygoing, he sold his jewelry store in 1913 and went to work for his affluent father-in-law.

Marx Straus (who as a retired capitalist preferred to be called Mark) died in 1912. August died in 1922. Their Oberlin careers are an authentic Horatio Alger success story: rags to riches.

WILLIAMS-WARD
HOUSE
335 East College

Charles Whiting Williams was a pioneer in adapting Oberlin's missionary impulse to the urban world of twentieth-century workingmen. An 1899 Oberlin graduate, he studied for the ministry in Berlin and Chicago before returning to be President Henry Churchill King's assistant from 1904 to 1912. During these years interurban electric transit made Oberlin a virtual Cleveland suburb. Williams perceived bright possibilities in this situation. He urged college students to use the city as a social laboratory for learning about the urban poor. Acting on his own precept, he left Oberlin to direct the Cleveland Federation for Charity and Philanthropy (now the Cleveland Welfare Federation). Later he became personnel manager for a Cleveland steel company.

In 1920 he took a bolder step toward communion with the masses. Quitting his managerial post, he assumed the identity and work clothes of "Charles Heitman," wage laborer. In this disguise he took a series of jobs in coal mines, steel mills, oil refineries, and railroad shops in order to discover, in his words, "what's on the worker's mind." His conclusion, reported in a stream of absorbing books published across the 1920s, was that workers were at bottom less interested in their paychecks than in finding a sense of worth and meaning in their working lives—"to be somebody." Life, he later generalized, was a "flight from futility." The message has an oddly durable ring.

Williams's Oberlin home was built on a wooded lot next to President King's house in 1910. Williams described it to a friend as "a sort of Italian cottage." The plans came from W. Dominick

183

Benes, a partner in the Cleveland architectural firm of Hubbell & Benes, which designed the Cleveland Art Museum in 1916. The house contains some of the finest living spaces in town. In 1917 Williams sold it to art historian and architect Clarence Ward. Ward lived here for over half a century, and left a lasting impress on college and town. In 1976 the Williams-Ward house became a group home for adults operated by the Lorain County Board of Mental Retardation.

KINNEY HOUSE
265 West College

Joseph Lyman Silsbee made a modest niche for himself in the architectural record of his time, not only as Frank Lloyd Wright's first professional mentor but as an inventive Midwestern practitioner of the Shingle Style. Most students of his career have him slipping into obscurity by the 1890s. Just when he slipped into Oberlin architectural history is not clear. He may have designed James Severance's house on South Professor Street in 1894. Eight years later Severance was his main liaison in the commission for the Memorial Arch on Tappan Square, and the main backer of his frustrated hopes for a square filled with Silsbee buildings. Men's Building (Wilder Hall) was his last work for the college.

In 1911, 14 months before his death, Silsbee completed this home for newspaper editor Carl W. Kinney. It suggests the elastic range of the architect's versatility. The Kinney house is Oberlin's closest brush with the Prairie School, several of whose practitioners, Wright included, worked in Silsbee's Chicago office in the late 1880s. Many hallmarks of the school are present here—smooth stucco walls over metal lathe, hip roof with broad sheltering eaves, open floor plan sweeping the interior from front to rear, fireplace and inglenook off to one side, clean plaster surfaces set off by dark woodwork throughout. The house creates a strong mood of airy privacy. Its third-floor dormers were added in the mid-1920s.

Kinney spent a long career in local journalism

185

and printing. A progressive young man, he started *The Owl* while still a schoolboy at the Oberlin academy, and edited the *Tribune* (which later merged into the *News-Tribune*) from 1899 to 1934. His son, Carl W. Kinney, Jr., then launched *The Times* to give the town its last choice of papers and editorial perspectives from 1936 to 1951.

In 1956 the Kinney house became home for German professor Joseph Reichard and his wife Anita, who was dean of women at the college in the late 1960s.

APOLLO THEATRE
19 East College

Despite stiff competition from college film series and the lure of Midway Mall and Avon
Lake, for most Oberlinians going to the movies
means the Apollo. It has been that way since
1928, when Jerry Steel came to town, bought
the Apollo, and turned it into a downtown en-
tertainment capital—Oberlin's small-town
answer to the exotic movie palaces of big-city
America.

Thomas Edison's moving picture show was
first exhibited in Oberlin in February 1900,
featuring blurry clips of yacht races, military
parades, and an imaginary trip to the moon.
Several commercial movie shows, supplemented
by vaudeville acts and hypnotists, opened here
and there, beginning in the space over Gibson's
bakery in 1907. In 1914 William Hobbs completed a new tan brick block on East College to
house his restaurant next to a modern 300-seat
movie house—the Apollo, George Broadwell,
proprietor. *Thor, Lord of the Jungle*, a three-reel
thriller, was its first community offering. For
years the Apollo competed with the Rex on
South Main for the money of a movie-hungry
town. But the morality of the craze seemed
dubious to custodians of village virtue. In the
early 1920s the local Parent-Teachers Association and the Daughters of the American Revolution cosponsored a drive for nicer movies.

187

Meanwhile the college began its own film nights in Finney Chapel.

Jerry Steel's arrival in Oberlin, and the advent of the "talkies," made commercial movies respectable again. Steel, born into a Cleveland family of entertainers, had fought with the American army in France during World War I, and managed the Alhambra Theatre, then Cleveland's largest, for a time before joining Warner Brothers as a distributor. Under his management the Apollo was steadily enlarged and modernized across the depression decade (boom years for American movies), and Zig-Zag Moderne became its primary decorative motif inside and out. The most recent major remodelling occurred in 1950, with the arrival of the triangular porcelain marquee with travelling neon lights, a new facade of shiny black glass, and interior walls of padded vinyl and glossy crimson velveteen.

When Jerry Steel died in 1959, his son Bill continued the family business. In the teeth of fast changes in film and television marketing, the Steel enterprise hung on, catering to the rival cinematic tastes of town and gown.

188

HENDERSON HOUSE
Route 10 East

Oberlin has harbored few Horatio Alger types across the years. Thomas Henderson was one of them. A canny Scot born in Glasgow in 1849, he came to the United States at age 30, learned the mechanic's trade, and landed in Cleveland in 1881. A decade later he entered partnership with Alexander Winton and married Winton's sister Catherine. Winton, also a Scottish immigrant, was a pioneer of the American automobile industry. Henderson became his right-hand man in the formation of the Winton Bicycle Company, later the Winton Motor Carriage Company, which began making Winton cars in 1897. (Oberlin saw its first automobile when Winton drove one of his machines through town in August 1899 on a test run from Cleveland to Chicago.)

Winton and Henderson were bold men in a risky young industry with an unknown future. Among those skeptical about the automobile was the B. F. Goodrich Company of Akron. One of Henderson's feats was to persuade Goodrich to experiment in manufacturing rubber tires for Winton's cars. The experiment worked.

In 1911 Henderson went into affluent early retirement as company vice-president, moved to Oberlin, and was soon made an Oberlin College trustee. His first Oberlin home, near the eastern edge of town on a stock farm called Sherrill Acres, burned in February 1917 while he and his wife were wintering in Florida. They

189

promptly hired Cleveland architect Charles W. Hopkinson to design a fireproof neo-Georgian mansion on the same site. It was a showpiece of the region, a vast stuccoed home of tile walls, with interior spaces of generous sweep finished in mahogany and oak. Gabled dormers lighted third-floor rooms, and terraced porches flanked the house on either side.

Henderson enjoyed his new home just seven years, selling it in 1924 shortly after his wife's death. (At about this time the Winton Company was absorbed by General Motors.) In 1965 his country estate became the home of Ann and Dayton Livingston, who revived farming and livestock operations on the surrounding acres. The place remains one of Oberlin's more romantic looking twentieth-century architectural assets.

**PRESIDENT'S HOUSE
154 Forest**

The town's most satisfying model of neo-Georgian architecture, this house has served as home for Oberlin College presidents since 1927. It was built for physics professor Samuel R. Williams and completed in the summer of 1920. Williams's faculty colleague Clarence Ward designed it and supervised its construction every step of the way. Contractor J. B. Tucker recalled that Ward's perfectionism ran up costs to the point where Williams wryly joked about his Forest Street folly. Faculty gossip hinted that the final bill came to four times what Williams intended. Ward, who came to Oberlin to head the art department in 1916, belonged to a breed now almost extinct. Today many architects enjoy doubling as theorists and critics, but few art historians try their hand as architects. Ward was clearly better versed in the building art of eighteenth-century New England than in the home construction business of twentieth-century Ohio. But the applause for his results outlived the gasps, and has been steady ever since.

The design recaptured the High Georgian goal of symmetrical repose imported to the American colonies through English pattern books. With its superbly proportioned hip roof and striking central pavilion defined by broad white pilasters against warm brick, the house bears resemblance to several distinguished domestic monuments dating from the years around 1760, including the Lady Pepperrell House in Kittery Point, Maine, and the Long-

191

fellow House in Cambridge, Massachusetts, both finished in wood. The style of the Forest Street doorway recalls the later Greek Revival era, however, and the interior room arrangements are strictly twentieth-century. Professor Williams lived in the house less than three years. After a leave of absence in California working with Nobel laureate Robert Millikan (an Oberlin graduate) on the nature of electricity, he left for Amherst College in 1924. Oberlin College bought the house three years later for $31,000 to make a home for Ernest Hatch Wilkins. Each succeeding presidential family—Stevensons, Carrs, Fullers, Danenbergs, and now the Starrs—has fitted the house with a special ambiance, closely monitored by faculty and staff.

In the 1920s the automobile went far to transform American culture and the American
landscape. Oberlin was not immune. A Winton
had rolled through town back in 1899. The
first villager to own a car, Dr. H. W. Pyle,
bought his Stanley Steamer a year later. But
early cars were expensive, erratic toys, and
many people regarded them as a threat—to
horses, trolleys, law and order, and to life itself. In 1910 the *Oberlin News* called them
"devil wagons," "the greatest enemy of the
public highways ever created."

Two decades later, the devil had clearly triumphed. Macadamized roads drew commuters
away from the ailing interurban trolley network. Model T collisions at downtown inter-
sections were commonplace. A new "white
way" lighted Main Street far into the night.
Necking parties became a problem along with
the crush of out-of-town cars arriving for Saturday afternoon college football games. By the
end of the 1920s Henry Ford rivalled Teddy
Roosevelt and Charles Lindbergh in the minds
of schoolboys and their fathers as the greatest
American who ever lived.

The businesses clustering at the intersection of
South Main and Vine felt the change most
sharply. This corner had long been geared to
transportation technology. Once crowded with
livery stables and blacksmith and buggy shops,
it acquired its first car storage garage in 1909.
On Saturday night, 14 September 1929—while
Clara Bow starred in *Dangerous Curves* at the
Apollo—Henry Klermund opened his new Ford

193

headquarters at 82 South Main, and over 2,000 townspeople attended a free dance on his salesroom floor.

Next door to the south, across from Wright Park, the Janby Oil Company began erecting its long-awaited "superstation" the following summer. Oberlin architect William B. Durand provided the plans. Featuring a two-car canopy for quick, convenient fill-ups, three service bays, and a sparkling ladies' room, Janby's was touted as one of the finest modern gas stations in this part of the state.

A similar station, built by Sicilian immigrant Joe Artino, went up simultaneously on East Lorain to serve motorists travelling through town on Route 20, the major transcontinental highway of the day connecting Boston to the Rockies by way of Oberlin.

Both stations sold gas at 19 cents a gallon. By the 1980s both were auto repair shops.

MALLORY HOUSE
58 East College

The site of one of the oldest dwellings in the village, this gracious house has undergone many remodellings and bears little resemblance to the original. The rough-hewn log beams in the basement are probably the oldest thing about it. William Ingersoll, a great-grandson of the theologian Jonathan Edwards, arrived in 1837 from Lee, Massachusetts, and moved into a house already built on this spot, then near the eastern edge of town. The Ingersoll family lived here until 1853 when they sold to Alanson Spooner and moved two blocks east on College. Shoe dealer Benjamin Locke, who bought the place from Spooner, drastically altered and expanded it in 1867. In 1879 he added a fancy crenelated wooden tower to the front facade. Toward the end of the century Locke became proprietor of Park House, the old Oberlin Inn. After his death his home began its long career as a college boarding hall.

In 1932 Mary Pope Mallory had the house completely remodelled by Oberlin architect William B. Durand. Durand restyled the place to give it a look reminiscent of the Federal era. He dismantled Locke's crenelated tower, introduced the present pedimented pavilion with recessed doorway, and repeated the round arch of the fanlight in decorative moldings over the first-floor windows and in the dormers piercing the hip roof. The remodelling later earned the house inclusion in a standard architectural survey of the Western Reserve as one of the fine early homes of Oberlin—an unwitting

195

tribute to the subtlety of Durand's work for Mrs. Mallory. She ran a boardinghouse until 1947 when the college purchased the building from her estate. Despite a somewhat offhanded application of wide-clapboard aluminum siding in 1970, Mallory remains among the better-looking buildings in downtown Oberlin.

MOULTON HOUSE
291 Forest

At first glance the dark red brick house on the corner of Forest and Prospect Streets looks to be yet another variation on the English Tudor cottage style which gained currency in the first decade of the twentieth century. The compact massing of its gables, along with the medieval references in the prominent front chimney, touches of half-timbering, narrow casement windows, and the Gothic arches in the woodwork of the small front porch, make it a pleasing, snug expression of that particular revival.

Appearances can be misleading. This is Oberlin's first steel-frame home. Designed by Cleveland architect Myron T. Hill and constructed by Steel-Bilt Homes, a Cleveland firm, it went up in the depression year 1932, when few other houses were being built in Oberlin. The client was Professor Gertrude Moulton of the college physical education department.

Steel-frame construction, while somewhat more costly than conventional wood framing, had many technical advantages. The joists of the floors are filled with concrete, with flooring of grained oak and maple laid over them. Interior walls are of metal lathe fastened to the frame, packed with insulation and finished in antiqued plaster. The result is a tight, fireproof, soundproof structure, cool in summer and economical in winter.

While it was going up, the house was also a threat—whether to unemployed carpenters in fear of new technology, or union men who

197

resented the contractor's use of non-union workers, is unclear. One night in early March 1932, when the steel frame stood naked in the dark, a carload of men pulled up, threw a heavy cable over a girder, and tried to pull it down. The frame held, the cable snapped, and the men fled. The incident was the talk of the town.

Construction proceeded and was completed by summer's end, when Prof. Moulton came home from the 1932 Olympic Games to settle in. She lived here with a group of other women physical education instructors for many years. Art historian Richard Spear and his wife, the artist Athena Tacha, bought the house in 1968.

The completion of the U.S. Post Office in April 1934 marked the architectural arrival of the federal government in Oberlin. During the first 60 years in the town's history, the post office moved from one downtown location to another, depending on the whereabouts of the current postmaster. More often than not he was a prominent lawyer or merchant, and a local leader of the party in power in Washington. The post office was the village nerve center, where men gathered to smoke, talk politics, swap gossip, and settle deals while towns-people and college students came by to pick up their daily mail. The advent of free home delivery in 1889 changed these patterns, and robbed the office of much of its social vitality. In later years, civil service reform gradually sapped its local political clout. The mail service, like so many other aspects of American life, was becoming bureaucratized, and politicos gave way to clerks.

From 1895 to 1934 the post office was housed in the Beckwith Block (since destroyed) just south of Union School House. The prospect of a new, modernized facility surfaced during Herbert Hoover's presidency, when federal building projects multiplied, anticipating the public construction boom of the New Deal years. Oberlin won its share of this patronage through the influence of college trustee Grove Patterson, editor of the *Toledo Blade* and a friend of Hoover's postmaster general, Walter Brown. The design came from Toledo architect

Alfred Hahn, also a friend of Patterson and Brown. Its quasi-classical exterior conformed to conventional federal guidelines for public architecture. Finished in tan brick trimmed with Kipton sandstone, and nicely landscaped, the building vastly improved the appearance of the South Main Street business district.

Big Jim Farley, Franklin Roosevelt's famous postmaster general, dropped by in 1937 to dedicate the place. His name is carved, somewhat misleadingly, on the cornerstone. Above the fluted Doric columns of the entry, the name of the building itself appears in metallic letters. The Post Office looks so much like a post office that these letters aren't really necessary. Like the federal bureaucracy it represents, the building is predictable and bland. But the people who work inside make it a friendly hometown place.

CERF HOUSE
373 Edgemeer

The years between the two world wars witnessed a revolution of building theory and technique, which had origins both in Europe and the early work of Frank Lloyd Wright. The first major American exhibition of the new architecture, called the International Style, was held in New York City in 1932. A year later William Hoskins Brown, a former Oberlin student fresh from architectural training at M.I.T., joined the Oberlin faculty. Brown brought the revolution to this village. His first local commission was this house, built in 1937 for Raymond Cerf, a Belgian-born, Paris-trained violin professor.

The house radiated the newness from every angle. Its severe rectilinear outline and unconventional fenestration widened neighbors' eyes and set tongues clucking. The architect later recalled that when the concrete shell of the house was completed, but with window openings still gaping unglazed, someone asked, "When do they mount the cannon?" A few years later the concrete block walls were sheathed with wooden clapboards to make the house more weatherproof and less stark in tone.

In retrospect Brown played down the important contribution he made to Oberlin's architectural development. "The arrival of 'Modern' at Oberlin was inevitable," he wrote in 1976. "Any momentum I may have added was through plugging the concept." He preferred the term "Functionalism" to define his purposes. Easy family traffic patterns, airy ventilation, natural lighting, and domestic privacy determined his living spaces. The corner windows and translucent glass brick panels of the Cerf house, so arresting when viewed from the street, were intended for internal convenience rather than external show. The house was planned from the inside out, and in the architect's mind at least, its visual message was incidental to its use.

Professor Cerf's domestic arrangements proved to be as cosmopolitan as his architectural taste. Complications in his marital affairs—which kept the faculty gossip mill churning overtime and provoked frowns among college administrators—spurred his departure from Oberlin in 1943.

SEAMAN HOUSE
158 South Prospect

The Cerf house on Edgemeer was not only an architectural benchmark in itself; it was a catalyst for the creation of a cluster of new houses at the nearby corner of Prospect and Morgan. In 1938 four couples bought adjoining lots there with the idea of asking William Hoskins Brown, the young architect of the Cerf house, to plan their homes. As it worked out after long negotiations, Brown designed houses for two of the families, the Seamans on Prospect and the Butlers on Morgan. At the corner between these two, Mr. and Mrs. John C. Kennedy ultimately carried out their own plans, and the fourth couple, the Steiners on Morgan, built after Brown had left Oberlin to join the M.I.T. faculty in 1941.

The Seaman house, completed just before his departure, is Brown's most important Oberlin legacy. Here the principles of functional architecture, which he championed in college assembly talks, local radio broadcasts, and countless private conversations, find mature expression: convenient multipurpose use of flowing interior space; continuity and adaptability in the composition of that space; and the absence of applied ornament. In this case, conventional wood frame technology is at work, but the functional arrangements—planned in close cooperation with the clients—make for radical aesthetic departures.

The bold flat roof plane, enforcing the horizontal bands of wide clapboard siding, makes the house seem to rest easily on its elevated ter-

203

raced setting. A profusion of right-angle set-backs and indentations, punctuated by window surprises at every turn, enliven the boxy design. A notable detail is the side location of the main entry near the garage, deferring to the convenience of the car.

William Seaman had been director of admissions at the college since 1928. An affable, charming, restless man, he enjoyed uncommon influence in the college community. His suicide in March 1948 was an enigmatic shock. His wife Fran ran a small nursery school here for a number of years after his death. The house belonged to Mr. and Mrs. Lewis R. Tower from 1957 to 1979. Well maintained and superbly landscaped, it remains a striking monument to the concept of the modern that arrived in the 1930s.

ARTZ HOUSE
157 North Professor

Frederick B. Artz was the most distinguished historian ever to teach at the college. Graduating from Oberlin in 1916, he returned to join the faculty in 1924, specializing in European intellectual and political history. A prolific author, he earned a reputation spanning two continents long before retiring in 1962. Locally he was known as Freddy, one of the most piercing wits in town.

He was also a great collector of books and antiques. In 1940 he had his Cape Cod cottage built to make a home for himself, his collections, and his close friend, psychology professor Raymond Stetson. Architect William Hoskins Brown collaborated with Artz in the design, Artz sketching out what he wanted and Brown developing the final drawings and blueprints. Brown had won quite a name for himself as a proponent of architectural modernism on the strength of his recently completed Cerf and Seaman houses. He later recalled that mutual friends wondered how he would adapt to Artz's more traditional tastes: "What would happen when an irresistible force met an immovable object?" In fact the match was smooth and creative, owing in part, as Brown remembered it, to the mediating skills of Professor Stetson, who told him, "Make it work, make it comfortable, detail it well, and let any stylistic or non-stylistic chips fall where they may."

Artz made the big decisions, and they worked. The large living room, lined with built-in bookcases, with a floor-to-ceiling window looking

205

out on a rear terrace, has been called the most beautiful room in Oberlin. Much of Artz's 14,000 volume private library filled this room. Graduates of his courses numbering in the thousands will long remember the splendid Sunday morning breakfast receptions he held here.

Musing over his career a few years before his death in 1983, Artz remarked, "I've written eleven books, but this house is my finest publication."

SOLDIERS MONUMENT Corner, Main and Vine

Oberlin's monument to its war dead dates from 1943, but the longer history of the memorial goes back to the Civil War. The original design, proposed by Professor Charles H. Churchill in 1868, called for a Gothic tower crowned by a small astronomical observatory. College trustees found this plan too costly. The monument completed in 1871 was a similar but less ambitious structure with marble commemorative tablets embedded at the base of a sandstone spire. It stood on college ground at the southeast corner of Professor and West College streets. Its twentieth-century fortunes oddly reflected shifting attitudes toward commemorating war.

By the early 1930s the memorial looked like a crumbling medieval ruin and was nicknamed "the sunken church." Most Civil War veterans had died. Gothic forms had fallen out of style, and patriotic sentiment ran low in the wake of World War I. At the Memorial Day observance of 1934, pacifist college students interrupted the village ceremony by laying antiwar placards ("Schools, Not Battleships," "Transfer All War Funds To Aid Of Needy Students") against the monument. A year later it was dismantled and its marble tablets placed in storage.

Then came World War II. Even before Pearl Harbor a drive got underway to build a new memorial at its present location away from the campus, overlooking Plum Creek in Wright

207

Park. William Hoskins Brown designed a simple terraced wall of old brick to hold tablets, including the originals, honoring the Oberlin casualties of all wars since 1861. This was dedicated in 1943.

Over the next three decades the wall began to tilt under the pressure from the embankment behind it. Corrective repairs were attempted after the Korean War. During the Vietnam War a drive to replace the wall with a new design ended in failure. Then in 1979 a city council decision to tear it down mobilized the local American Legion post to save it. The restoration project, headed by Carl Breuning, was complete in time for the town's sesquicentennial celebration of 1983.

The monument remembers 96 casualties (town and college) of the Civil War, 11 townsmen killed in World War I, 16 in World War II, and 2 each in Korea and Vietnam.

ARNOLD HOUSE
396 Morgan

Mr. Blandings Builds His Dream House, a 1946 bestseller, helped readers laugh their way through a widespread postwar urge to make a home of your own by Doing It Yourself. A few people actually did it. Among them were Paul and Sally Arnold, who created the first version of this house in 1948.

Paul Arnold graduated from the college in 1940. A year later, when William Hoskins Brown left the art department for M.I.T., Arnold was hired to replace him. He had taken Brown's course in architectural design, which turned out to be handy when he returned from military service after the war with his wife Sally (also an Oberlin graduate) and began to plot their dream house.

Central to their planning was the concept of split-level family space organized around a bedroom balcony overlooking a high-ceilinged living room. Arnold worked their ideas to the blueprint stage and cleared them with a professional architect, Franklin Scott of Berea. Then he went to work in the summer of 1948 helping contractor Lee Ross build the house. Adequate building materials were still hard to come by that soon after the war, but Arnold found them, including a fine lot of wormy chestnut for wall siding and sandstone for his fireplace culled from the Kipton quarry. The house was almost ready when the Arnolds moved in to celebrate Christmas.

They liked what they had made but soon found

it was not enough for a family of six. It became the core of a molecular home that grew incrementally over the years, a spatial collage in the best tradition of early American additive architecture. The garage turned into a dining room; a rear porch became a music room, with a new porch beyond that; and the front porch was enclosed for an entry hall. Every detail reflected the choice and talent of its owners.

The Arnolds employed the Do-It-Yourself ethic to create one of Oberlin's most innovative homes. Twenty-two years later James and Janice Thibo moved in nearby, at 344 Morgan. Thibo, a mason from Avon, Ohio, spent a year doing his new house, a little gambrel-roofed brick cottage which looks like something out of colonial Williamsburg, neat, complete, and contained. He made it with the bricks from an abandoned country schoolhouse on Hamilton Street west of town, once used by a local farmer for storing pigs.

Together the Arnold and Thibo homes, one experimenting with the future, the other reaching for the past, suggest the latitude of possibilities still open for those tempted to try out their own dreams. Products of twentieth-century hand craftsmanship, they keep alive the thrifty tactics used for shelter when Oberlin was still a clearing in the woods.

210

WELTZHEIMER-JOHNSON HOUSE
127 Woodhaven

Thanks to the thoughtful enterprise of two women, Mrs. Charles Weltzheimer and Professor Ellen Johnson, Oberlin is the proud possessor of the first Frank Lloyd Wright Usonian house in Ohio.

The Usonian idea was Wright's response to the architectural challenge posed for affluent Americans by the Great Depression and the graduated income tax. A simplification of his earlier Prairie Style homes, it pared the concept of the house to lean and elemental terms while promoting Wright's vision of a nation of families scattered broadcast over the landscape close to nature. Garage, basement, gutters, downspouts, paint, plaster, excess furniture, and fancy trim vanished from the pure Usonian house. So did the formal dining room. Informal, multipurpose family space, framed by warm walls of brick and redwood, generous fenestration, and cantilevered roofs, governed the appearance. Its arrangements provided many inspirations for the modern ranch-style home. Wright's earliest Usonian house went up in Madison, Wisconsin, in 1937.

A decade later Mrs. Weltzheimer, wife of a prospering auto dealer, asked the architect to design a home for a large lot on Oberlin's western edge. The resulting plan is firmly grounded in the Usonian vein. Wright's open spatial flow through kitchen, fireplace, and living room ends in the long low-ceilinged channel of the bedroom corridor. The ornamentation along the clerestory and eaves of this wing is unique

211

among Usonian homes. The house was built under the supervision of a Wright apprentice, Theodore Bower, between 1948 and 1950. Oriented toward the sun and the land rather than the city's street grid, it hugged its flat, once lonely site with intimate grace.

After the Weltzheimers' departure, the house met with poor treatment, and neighboring suburban homes began to crowd it. In 1968, Oberlin art professor Ellen Johnson took ownership. With the help of contractor Glenn Hobbs, Jr., she launched a careful restoration, requiring several years of painstaking work and sensitive attention to detail. Her home now promises to remain a lasting local monument to America's greatest twentieth-century architect.

College Park, better known today as Shipherd Circle (named after Oberlin's founder), was the town's first post-World War II planned residential development. It originated in the urgent need for good housing to attract and retain high-quality college faculty members in the teeth of postwar inflation. President William Stevenson noted this need soon after his arrival in 1946. To help meet it, the college acquired a large tract of land on the eastern edge of town south of East College Street, the acreage long known as Caskey farm, once owned by William Caskey, who taught oratory at the college from 1898 to 1919.

The Federal Housing Authority provided a curvilinear street plan for the site, free of sidewalks in deference to the automobile. Street paving and utilities costs were eased by a college loan, and half the lots marked out were reserved for sale to college faculty and staff.

The earliest homes on the southern arc of the circle proved to be among the most daring in appearance. Their construction began in 1950. The first to be completed, at 220 Shipherd Circle, belonged to Professor Harold Fildey of the graduate school of theology. It was designed by Max Ratner and Douglas Johnson, in what they called the "contemporary" style—distinguished by a low, flaring butterfly roof with wide eaves shading ribbon windows. The exterior walls, rising from a concrete pad, are

213

sheathed with vertical redwood planks which have weathered to a tawny brown.

The Fildey house was one of several modern Oberlin homes designed by Ratner and Johnson in the early 1950s. The first batch on Shipherd Circle absorbed a good deal of hand labor from their owners—Professors Fildey, Marie Rankin, William Hellmuth, and Dean Blair Stewart—who called themselves "Builders Collaborative" and pooled resources to cut costs.

When the theology school closed in 1966, Fildey sold his home to David and Chloe Young and moved to Vanderbilt University. Three decades after its construction, the house retains a bold experimental look.

The Shipherd Circle development, with 67 homes in all today, is an eclectic sampling of middle-class domestic housing tastes as they have evolved over the past thirty years. Like its analogue on the western side of town, Robin Park, it is Oberlin's version of a distinctive American invention—ground-hugging homes in an enclave of curving streets with broad lawns flowing unimpeded into one another, broken only by their driveways: the modern automobile suburb.

In February 1960 seven children died on Lincoln Street when flames from a leaking oil heater destroyed the shack they lived in with their mothers, two sisters on welfare. The city had turned off their electricity three weeks earlier because of unpaid bills. The fire exposed the village conscience to a reality long neglected—the ramshackle state of low-income private housing in the southeast quadrant, where most blacks in Oberlin lived.

The community moved with earnest speed to mend this situation. City manager Richard Dunn accelerated condemnations of houses unfit for habitation. Private loan programs for modest home improvements were launched. In 1961 the city council passed a fair housing ordinance to ban discrimination in housing sales and rentals. And a housing renewal commission, chaired by Robert Thomas, went to work exploring remedies in the public sector. This last initiative resulted in Oberlin's low-income pagoda houses—54 units of them built in 1965 and 1966 in seven separate locations. The largest cluster is located on Berger Court off East Lorain. The units were financed by loans from the federal Public Housing Authority, and designed by Meathe, Kessler & Associates of Grosse Pointe, Michigan. Their scattered siting aimed to escape the ghetto image fixed in many minds by the concentrated big-city housing projects of the day. To allay fears that Oberlin's public housing might attract poor families

215

from elsewhere, a year's residence was required for eligibility.

Some people thought that the units' peculiar
rooflines (which hid vents, chimneys, and sky-
lights) made them too easily identified. Still,
for most Oberlinians the pagoda houses helped
blunt guilt and promote pride. Occupants
seemed satisfied with their new lodgings.
Complaints centered on periodic inspections,
cramped storage space for dryers, power lawn
mowers, and other possessions, and too much
white paint on interior walls. Despite these
drawbacks, a long waiting list soon developed,
and turnover was slow. By 1970 not a single
family had left because of excess income. One
happy resident explained, "It is a nice new
home, and I intend to stay here for the rest of
my life."

**JOHN FREDERICK
OBERLIN
APARTMENTS
138 South Main**

For well over a century, the young and the old have loomed large in Oberlin's population profile. The college and its preparatory department accounted for the original accent on youth. The calm pace of village life and its low-cost amenities, plus fond memories of days gone by, attracted the elderly. Their numbers began rising after the Civil War. For example, by one count 17 widows lived on one block of Cedar Street in 1885. Seventy years later newspaper editor Charles Mosher noted that old age rest homes were the town's fastest growing industry, and warned that many of them were antique wooden firetraps stalked by potential disaster.

When the 1960 Lincoln Street fire triggered a move toward modern public housing, concern for the welfare of the aged entered the formula for reform. Half the units authorized by the federal Public Housing Authority were designated as apartments for the elderly. Meathe, Kessler & Associates, designers of Oberlin's scattered-site pagoda housing, were also chosen as architects for the apartment building by a selection committee that included artist Paul Arnold and architect Douglas Johnson. Arnold cited "distinction in appearance" as a major virtue of the high-rise complex, the town's first "skyscraper," which went up on South Main above Plum Creek in 1965–66. It is named for John Frederick Oberlin, the Alsatian minister after whom John Shipherd named the town back in 1833.

J.F.O.'s smooth tan brick walls, the staggered elevations in its massing, and the random scattering of its tall pucker-framed windows gave

217

it by all odds the most interesting exterior of the three large apartment buildings constructed in the 1960s. The others are the Firelands Retirement Center on South Pleasant financed by the United Church of Christ, and the College Park Manor on East College, which caters to affluent adults of all ages.

**ALLEN MEMORIAL
HOSPITAL
200 West Lorain**

Before Oberlin's first rudimentary hospital opened at 21 South Cedar in 1907, people in need of medical care were either treated at home or taken to Cleveland. The Cedar Street infirmary was inadequate the day it opened. As early as 1914 hospital trustees bought land for a modern facility on West Lorain, where Allen Memorial Hospital stands today.

Dudley Peter Allen, an Oberlin "townie" who graduated from the college in 1875, had followed his father's path to medicine and spent his career as a Cleveland surgeon. Marriage into the oil-rich Severance family grounded him on Millionaire's Row among Cleveland's Euclid Avenue elite. A cultivated philanthropist, he deeded the money that created both his alma mater's art museum and his hometown's hospital. Allen's widow, Elizabeth Severance Allen, announced the gift for the hospital in

219

1916, asking that its name honor both her husband and his father.

Negotiations over the project inched forward over the next eight years, delayed by war, postwar inflation, and disputes over appearance and size. Finally a fresh gift from Allen's widow, and a scaled-down one-story design from architect Cass Gilbert, prompted construction in 1924–25.

Gilbert's hospital, set back far from the street to anticipate future expansion, was perhaps his most picturesque Oberlin creation—a long, low building of red tile roofs and white stuccoed walls, decorated with colorful medallions and entry lunettes. An easy village atmosphere pervaded the place. For lucky patients, windowsill visiting hours might occur at any time, day or night.

The 1925 hospital, owned by the college while serving the whole community, sufficed till 1954, when ownership passed from college to city, and a central wing was added to the north, doubling bed capacity. In 1960 a nonprofit corporation assumed control of the facility, and two years later the Oberlin Clinic opened next door to the west. Then in 1970, construction began on a big new two-story bunker-shaped hospital addition of tan brick, designed by a Kansas City firm, Hewitt & Royer. This doubled capacity again, and brought Oberlin abreast of medical modernization one more time. Gilbert's hospital was swallowed up in the expansion, but on either side of the latest version, relics of his original exterior design can still be seen.

Since 1833 Oberlinians have not been allowed to forget the main reason for their town, or its main employer. "Oberlin's great manufacturing plant," President King once reminded local businessmen, "happens to be a college." The creation of an industrial park at the northeastern corner of town in 1959 brought some important supplements after a long search. Among the light industries that gathered there, Gilford Instrument Lab has knitted itself into the life of the community most closely.

The search for economic diversity started over a century before, with experiments in furniture and silkworms. After the Civil War, a restless growth psychology gripped local townsmen along with the rest of the country. "In this go-ahead age," the village editor urged in 1871, "Oberlin must either bestir itself or be left far in the background by its more enterprising neighbors. Let us manufacture something besides brains, if it is only toothpicks." Oil, natural gas, lumber, and glass each had their local boomers. In 1881 the editor noted that new train lines were passing Oberlin by. Elsewhere, he reported, they were "making hundreds of people wild with joy in anticipation of having a railroad at their own doors." "Why cannot Oberlin have a railroad excitement?" he wondered.

From 1890 till 1940 Oberlin grew hardly at all. Meanwhile Elyria took off, and villagers called the pink glow of Lorain's new steel mills in the

221

evening sky their "Northern Lights." By 1911 the local paper was getting a little hysterical: "Let us keep on putting in our best licks for the town, and always give out the impression that the town is growing and there is room here for more capital, more houses, and more people, and keep on forever talking that way." In the 1920s a calmer mood prevailed, despite evidence that local young people were leaving in droves to look for jobs. "We have nothing to offer in the way of inducements for industries to locate here," the mayor confessed. "It is strictly an educational and residential place, and in my judgment will remain so for many years to come." The paper now contented itself with calling Oberlin "the Garden Spot of Ohio" and offering "concrete proof of our Normalcy."

The 1950 census found the town growing for the first time in decades. Rezoning for light industry became a hot political item. By 1959 the most aggressive and progressive local businessman, Bill Long, manager of the Oberlin Consumer Cooperative, had formed a community development organization to stimulate orderly growth. An industrial park was laid out off East Lorain, and Long announced plans for a Pepperidge Farm bakery and a federal air traffic control center to locate here. As it turned out, Pepperidge Farm never showed up, and air control center employees from Detroit and Pittsburgh mostly preferred to live elsewhere. But meanwhile Saul Gilford brought his small lab for making medical research instruments to the park.

Gilford, a New Yorker trained at M.I.T., had worked at the National Bureau of Standards and then founded his own firm in Elyria before coming to Oberlin. He arrived in 1959 with ten employees. Three years later his operations had doubled in size, and the first of many plant additions went up. The most prominent of them, an office complex of tan brick, white aggregate and dark glass, was produced by Danon, Worley, Cady, Kirk & Associates of Cleveland in 1971. By then the work force was up to 600. Gilford practiced affirmative action in local hiring long before it became public policy. He received the college's Distinguished Community Service Award in 1977. On 17 November 1979, he took off in his twin engine Cessna with his wife Mikie Sherman and her daughter Catharine for a flight to New England. They crashed in the night against Bald Mountain near Bennington, Vermont.

FIRE STATION
430 South Main

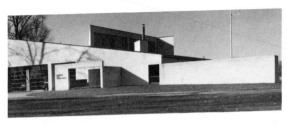

Oberlin celebrated an ancient and honorable American tradition by opening its new fire station on the country's bicentennial birthday, the Fourth of July, 1976. Volunteer bucket brigades and hook-and-ladder teams could be traced deep into the local past, their colorful histories a source of lusty pride. But nostalgia was one thing, and efficiency another. By the 1960s, modern fire-fighting technology had made existing facilities for equipment storage and readiness sadly obsolete. The big red trucks scraped in and out of their berths in the old city hall on South Main with scant inches to spare, and firemen on duty worked in what they called "the cave." Downtown traffic congestion was another hazard for the crews.

When city council members decided to build a new station on the southern edge of town—Oberlin's first municipal building since 1919—they also decided on a class act, "not just a brick box with a whistle on top." Cleveland architects Robert Barclay and William Blunden did their best. Taken by triangles, they offered a long low wedge of white-faced brick with big punctuations of tinted glass. The tall end of the wedge provided ample bays for fire trucks, with convenient drive-through access. Another high, sharp triangle, a tower for drying hoses, intersected the main wedge at a right angle, lending a touch of dramatic tension to the design. What the station achieved was space for easy movement on quick notice for its users and a striking introduction to the city for travelers. Council chairman Kinzer Habecker spoke for most townsmen when he cut the building's ribbon on Independence Day and yelled "Yahoo!"

NEW CITY HALL
85 South Main

In the early 1970s two rival strategies for municipal revival attracted urban planners. One involved city sponsorship of bright experiments in contemporary architecture along lines pioneered by Columbus, Indiana. The other called for recycling older buildings to combine historic preservation with adaptive reuse, as in Medina, Ohio. After a decade of strenuous debate, Oberlin veered toward a middle course, more or less.

The old city hall at 69 South Main, a plain expedient built in 1919 to replace its more ornate predecessor from the Gilded Age, had long dampened everyone's civic enthusiasm. When plans to expand it came before city council in 1970, one member dismissed them with the apt phrase, "Early Ugly." Meanwhile the idea of renovating old Union School House (Westervelt Hall) for city use surfaced and resurfaced for several years, but never quite captured majority imagination. Ambitious schemes for a large new municipal center, combining space for firemen, police, politicians, clerks, and (in one version) public housing were rejected by tax-conscious voters. Then city manager Tom Dalton nudged the council toward remodelling an abandoned food store to create more city office space. Architects William Blunden and Robert Barclay, fresh from acceptance of their new fire station, came in with imaginative plans for this transformation. They incorporated the roof and most walls of the old building but designed it out of recognition in a crisp modern format. Impressed by this solution, council proceeded to authorize a triangular addition to it just to the south. Before long, enough municipal services had migrated down the street to justify the term, "new city hall," leaving only the police behind in the old 1919 building.

The architects managed a look of outward coherence for their creation by surfacing exterior walls with a uniform plastic stucco. Inside, a mix of blond oak woodwork, heather carpeting, and red tile floors made for texture and warmth. An unusual new landscape enhanced the immediate environment, meandering east from the building toward Plum Creek and Athena Tacha's outdoor step sculpture.

As the project neared completion in 1977, and city council members prepared to move in, they were clearly ready to bask a while in their Fabian triumph. The only serious disappointment they discovered was that their seats in the bright new council chamber did not tilt back.

This ends the survey, but not the story. In the late 1970s the college entered a long pause in its building program, and began learning to pay more attention to what it has than to what it lacks. The pace of city growth has greatly slowed since the heady years from 1945 to 1965, when suburban sprawl spread the city well beyond the historic limits of the village. Meanwhile the great world of architecture has been spinning at a quicker clip than ever in the past. The record of both college and town suggests that if and when the time for growth arrives again, Oberlinians may be hard pressed to pull themselves toward newness in the building art. But in their own peculiar ways they will surely try.

NOTE ON SOURCES

This book is based almost entirely on primary evidence, drawn from a wide variety of sources, most of them local. Information about college buildings is available in abundance. Much of it is located in the Oberlin College Library and the Oberlin College Archives. The records in the archives are particularly dense and well organized. The papers of succeeding college presidents from King to Carr, records from the treasurer's office, and minutes of trustee meetings and the college prudential committee are rewarding. A large collection of plans, drawings, and blueprints of college buildings is located in the physical plant construction office in the Service Building.

The small batch of Cass Gilbert personal papers in the Manuscripts Division, Library of Congress, Washington, D.C., and the huge mass of his professional papers in the New-York Historical Society, New York City, are valuable for the Gilbert years.

Gathering good information about buildings in the town is a more chancy task. Sometimes it is easy, and at other times it is almost impossible. There is nothing logical or conclusive about it, but the serendipity along the way makes it great fun. Local newspapers are an excellent source, though coverage of local house construction over the years is inevitably uneven. Of the many local papers available in the original or on microfilm, the most convenient are the *Lorain County News* (1860-73), *Oberlin Weekly News* (1874-91), *Oberlin News* (1891-1930), and *Oberlin News Tribune* (1930-present). Manuscript census returns for 1840, 1850, 1860, 1870, 1880, 1900, and 1910, available on microfilm, provide useful biographical information about local residents, drawn from door-to-door surveys by census takers. City street directories, issued at varying intervals from 1859 to 1956, are helpful for determining who occupied what addresses at certain times. They tell nothing about the buildings at these addresses, however, and nothing about ownership.

The chain of ownership for a building and the property it occupies can be traced at the county auditor's office in Elyria. Anyone unfamiliar with the process of title search from grantor to grantee will find the people working at the auditor's office wonderfully friendly and helpful. Once the original property owner (grantee) has been established, the precise year of building construction can be discovered by checking the county tax records for the years in question. When the tax assessment for a parcel jumps decisively, that is strong evidence that construction occurred on the parcel in the previous year—even though the record will often indicate only an "h" (for house) as explicit reference to what was built. Later additions and improvements can be inferred from subsequent changes in tax assessment.

None of these records is foolproof. In the 1890s an enterprising man named L. B. Sperry came to Oberlin, built several houses on South Professor, and searched the title to several more. His testimony about his research in local building history, reported in the *Oberlin News*, 10 September 1901, conveys an exasperation worth noting:

> The title to some of our real estate is not ideal. . . . The lines of our streets and of our individual lots are so uncertain that neither lawyers nor surveyors can determine just "where we are at." . . . It is to be regretted that the early residents and

officials of Oberlin did not have a little more business foresight and worldy wisdom in laying out the town and providing for its enlargement. We of this generation have inherited some unpleasant conditions from the carelessness of our predecessors, a carelessness so grave as to fall little short of criminality. . . . If some of them had spent less time studying "the divine will" and seeking "personal salvation" in "the world to come," and put more time into seeking the establishment of correct landmarks, exact boundary lines, clear titles, and the legal rights of their neighbors in this world, it would have contributed much to the best welfare of coming generations. This world is so vast and so varied in its interests, that only a part of its problems can be settled in prayer meeting. . . . There are some details that Jesus did not undertake. They were left for us to do.

For the historian, as distinct from the realtor, the compensation is that in many cases the written record of ownership, construction, and residence can be supplemented by human memory after the fact. The local folk tradition is valuable both as hard evidence of historical reality and as a window on what is believed about the past. Whether it comes in written form or as oral testimony, however, it must be constantly tested against other kinds of evidence before it is credited as fact. If one is lucky, the accumulation of clues from as many sources as possible will add up to pretty conclusive proof of what really happened.

Finally the buildings themselves offer testimony which can be looked at and evaluated directly if they survive. Happily, Oberlin's relatively slow pace of growth has made for a survival rate higher than that of most American cities. Much has disappeared, but the best evidence about Oberlin's architectural past still lines its shaded streets.

BUILDINGS BY LOCATION

Building locations are here listed by street. The streets are in alphabetical order. Each entry includes the street number, the building name, and the page of this book on which a description of the building can be found. College buildings generally do not have numbered addresses.

233

INDEX

234

236